G000141536

Companion to the Sunday Gospels

Year A

by
Henry Wansbrough, OSB

*All booklets are published thanks to the
generous support of the members of the
Catholic Truth Society*

CATHOLIC TRUTH SOCIETY

PUBLISHERS TO THE HOLY SEE

ISBN 978 1 78469 137 0

The calling of Matthew reminds us that when Christ makes us his disciples, he does not look to our past but to the future. We need but respond to his call with a humble and sincere heart.

Pope Francis, General Audience, 13 April 2016

Jesus said to his disciples: 'As it was in Noah's day, so will it be when the Son of Man comes. For in those days before the Flood people were eating, drinking, taking wives, taking husbands, right up to the day Noah went into the ark, and they suspected nothing till the Flood came and swept all away. It will be like this when the Son of Man comes. Then of two men in the fields one is taken, one left; of two women at the millstone grinding, one is taken, one left.

'So stay awake, because you do not know the day when your master is coming. You may be quite sure of this that if the householder had known at what time of the night the burglar would come, he would have stayed awake and would not have allowed anyone to break through the wall of his house. Therefore, you too must stand ready because the Son of Man is coming at an hour you do not expect.'

Like a Thief in the Night

In each year of the three-year cycle the Advent Sunday Gospel readings have the same pattern: the first is about the final Coming of Christ. In the second John the Baptist is preparing a community of repentance to welcome Jesus's mission. In the third John the Baptist points out Jesus as the Messiah. On the fourth Sunday we look to Mary, preparing for the birth of her Son. In this Sunday's reading about the Second Coming the accent is the same as in the Pauline letter: a pressing and urgent need to take action without delay. The Second Coming will be sudden and unexpected, and will seem as random as the threat of one taken, one left, or as a thief in the night when no protective preparations have been made. We do not even know whether the final confrontation, when each of us is brought face to face with the awesome presence of God, will be a unique event for each of us at death, or whether it will be a group event, as in Matthew's parable of the sheep and goats sent to right and left. There is no time in eternity, no waiting-room! It will not be as any human mind can envisage it.

Question: Should we look forward to or dread the final meeting with the Lord?

In due course John the Baptist appeared; he preached in the wilderness of Judaea and this was his message: 'Repent, for the kingdom of heaven is close at hand.' This was the man the prophet Isaiah spoke of when he said:

> A voice cries in the wilderness:
> Prepare a way for the Lord,
> make his paths straight.

This man John wore a garment made of camel-hair with a leather belt round his waist, and his food was locusts and wild honey. Then Jerusalem and all Judaea and the whole Jordan district made their way to him, and as they were baptised by him in the river Jordan they confessed their sins. But when he saw a number of Pharisees and Sadducees coming for baptism he said to them, 'Brood of vipers, who warned you to fly from the retribution that is coming? But if you are repentant, produce the appropriate fruit, and do not presume to tell yourselves, "We have Abraham for our father," because, I tell you, God can raise children for Abraham from these stones. Even now the axe is laid to the roots of the trees, so that any tree which fails to produce good fruit will be cut down and thrown on the fire. I baptise you in water for repentance, but the one who follows me is more powerful than I am, and I am not fit to carry his sandals; he will baptise you with the Holy Spirit and fire. His winnowing-fan is in his hand; he will clear his threshing-floor and gather his wheat into the barn; but the chaff he will burn in a fire that will never go out.'

John the Baptist's Call to Repentance

'Repentance' is an unattractive idea. It conjures up morose brooding over past sins and failures, a negative idea. This is not what John the Baptist proclaimed. His message was wholly positive. In Hebrew and Greek the concept is a change of behaviour, a change of direction. John is calling on them to change their ways, to change their scale of values, their whole direction of life. To reinforce his message he wears the clothes worn by Elijah, the prophet who was to return to announce the final coming of the Lord. He proclaims his message in the desert, that apocalyptic landscape of the arid and bare Jordan Valley, below sea level, where merchants would be crossing the Jordan on the road to the East. So he makes a deliberate claim to be this final prophet and to be preparing a way for the Lord. We see Jesus as the Messiah, the loving Saviour, but John was not yet proclaiming Jesus. He was proclaiming the threatening and imminent arrival of the sovereignty of God, when rotten trees would be cut down and evil swept away to be burnt in unquenchable fire. If we are to be open to the arrival of the Kingship of God, we may need to look to our scale of values. Am I the only person who matters to me?

Question: Is my scale of values compatible with the Kingship of God? How far do they coincide?

John in his prison had heard what Christ was doing and he sent his disciples to ask him, 'Are you the one who is to come, or have we got to wait for someone else?' Jesus answered, 'Go back and tell John what you hear and see; the blind see again, and the lame walk, lepers are cleansed, and the deaf hear, and the dead are raised to life and the Good News is proclaimed to the poor; and happy is the man who does not lose faith in me.'

As the messengers were leaving, Jesus began to talk to the people about John: 'What did you go out into the wilderness to see? A reed swaying in the breeze? No? Then what did you go out to see? A man wearing fine clothes? Oh no, those who wear fine clothes are to be found in palaces. Then what did you go out for? To see a prophet? Yes, I tell you, and much more than a prophet: he is the one of whom scripture says: Look, I am going to send my messenger before you; he will prepare your way before you. I tell you solemnly, of all the children born of women, a greater than John the Baptist has never been seen; yet the least in the kingdom of heaven is greater than he is.'

Miracles of the Messiah

John the Baptist was expecting a Messiah of judgement, who would cut down the rotten tree and burn the useless chaff. When, in prison, he hears that Jesus is not doing this, he is puzzled and sends messengers to ask if Jesus is really the Messiah. Jesus sends back the message that he is fulfilling the prophet Isaiah - the passage which we heard in the first reading. Jesus's concept of the task of the Messiah was healing, not punishment. He goes and seeks out those who need both physical and moral healing. He does not wait for sinners to repent before gathering them in; he makes the first advance. Then he turns to praising the Baptist. It is a fascinating speculation whether Jesus was himself once a disciple of John the Baptist. After all, John says he did not recognise Jesus until he saw the Spirit coming down on him. He also says that Jesus, who came after him, has passed before him. This is a typical position of a rabbi, leading his disciples, and suggests that John had been Jesus's rabbi, then became his disciple. Jesus was fully man, and even he needed to learn as all human beings do.

This is how Jesus Christ came to be born. His mother Mary was betrothed to Joseph; but before they came to live together she was found to be with child through the Holy Spirit. Her husband Joseph, being a man of honour and wanting to spare her publicity, decided to divorce her informally. He had made up his mind to do this when the angel of the Lord appeared to him in a dream and said, 'Joseph son of David, do not be afraid to take Mary home as your wife, because she has conceived what is in her by the Holy Spirit. She will give birth to a son and you must name him Jesus, because he is the one who is to save his people from their sins.' Now all this took place to fulfil the words spoken by the Lord through the prophet:

> The virgin will conceive and give birth to a son
> and they will call him Emmanuel,

a name which means 'God-is-with-us'. When Joseph woke up he did what the angel of the Lord had told him to do: he took his wife to his home.

Emmanuel

Matthew begins his Gospel about the birth of Jesus with a long and elaborately formal genealogy of Joseph. But Jesus is the son of Mary, not of Joseph! The whole point of this story is that Joseph is not the genealogical father of Jesus, but adopts Jesus into his line of David. At first he is hesitant to do so, presumably thinking that he is unworthy to acknowledge the child as his own, and unworthy to bond with Mary who is with child by the Holy Spirit. But the angel insists ('Do not be afraid') that only Joseph can do this job. As soon as the child is born, he is given the name Jesus, and given it by Joseph. It is the father's prerogative to name a son, and by so doing Joseph takes the child as his own. We hear little more of Joseph, but what a joy it must have been to have Jesus as a son! What a relationship there must have been! What responsibility too! When Jesus calls God his 'Father', he is using the concept which must have been formed in his mind by his adoptive father, Joseph, the perfect ideal of the loving father.

Question: What did Jesus and Joseph talk about as they walked to work together?

In the beginning was the Word:
the Word was with God
and the Word was God.
He was with God in the beginning.
Through him all things came to be,
not one thing had its being but through him.
All that came to be had life in him
and that life was the light of men,
a light that shines in the dark,
a light that darkness could not overpower.
The Word was the true light
that enlightens all men;
and he was coming into the world.
He was in the world
that had its being through him,
and the world did not know him.
He came to his own domain
and his own people did not accept him.
But to all who did accept him
he gave power to become children of God,
to all who believe in the name of him
who was born not out of human stock
or urge of the flesh
or will of man
but of God himself.
The Word was made flesh,
he lived among us,
and we saw his glory,
the glory that is his as the only Son of the Father,
full of grace and truth.

The Word Made Flesh

The Prologue of St John has a special place in Christian theology, and for centuries was recited at the end of the Mass as summing up the whole work of redemption. It begins with God's creation by the Word, and ends with the completion of the purpose of creation through the grace and truth of Jesus Christ. In the centre comes the incarnation, which enables and invites those who accept Christ to become children of God. The Gospel story of Mark begins at the Baptism of Jesus, and the voice from heaven declaring that he is God's Son. Matthew and Luke add the infancy stories to show that Jesus possessed and manifested these divine qualities right from his birth. John goes back beyond this, to meditate on the ultimate part in both creation and its fulfilment of the Word who became flesh. Perhaps the most exultant cry of all is 'we have seen his glory', for glory belongs rightly to God alone. This statement contains the paradox that Christ as a human being made visible this divine glory, and that it was his own glory, witnessed by the followers among whom he lived and moved. It is their tradition that will be expressed in the Gospel story which follows and is celebrated through the year.

Question: What does 'we have seen his glory' mean?

(Longer form John 1:1-18)

The shepherds hurried away to Bethlehem and found Mary and Joseph, and the baby lying in the manger. When they saw the child they repeated what they had been told about him, and everyone who heard it was astonished at what the shepherds had to say. As for Mary, she treasured all these things and pondered them in her heart. And the shepherds went back glorifying and praising God for all they had heard and seen; it was exactly as they had been told.

When the eighth day came and the child was to be circumcised, they gave him the name Jesus, the name the angel had given him before his conception.

The Child in the Cattle Trough

The cosy picture of the bright-eyed child in the clean wooden manger (with the ox and the ass peeping in from a respectful distance) is misleading. The picture is one of destitution. There was no room for the newborn in the normal living quarters, and the worried mother had to lodge him in the only space available: a feeding trough for cattle, perched on top of their fodder. That was where the ragged sheep minders found him. They too were the poorest of the poor, no sheep of their own, just hired for the night. Perhaps they got a drink of goats' milk or a crust of bread for their shivering pains. Matthew does at least have the baby worshipped by those rather splendid Wise Men from the East, with their noble and symbolic gifts. No gifts forthcoming from today's rough crew. As we worry about our post-Christmas waistlines, and set out on our prosperous New Year, it makes us reflect on where true blessedness lies, and who are the chosen ones of the Lord. Surely God could have rustled up more suitable worshippers for his Incarnate Son than these scruffy down-and-outs? No, I'm afraid not.

Question: Why is the material destitution of Mary and Jesus so strongly stressed?

After Jesus had been born at Bethlehem in Judaea during the reign of King Herod, some wise men came to Jerusalem from the east. 'Where is the infant king of the Jews?' they asked. 'We saw his star as it rose and have come to do him homage.' When King Herod heard this he was perturbed, and so was the whole of Jerusalem. He called together all the chief priests and the scribes of the people, and enquired of them where the Christ was to be born. 'At Bethlehem in Judaea,' they told him 'for this is what the prophet wrote:

And you, Bethlehem, in the land of Judah
you are by no means least among the leaders of Judah,
for out of you will come a leader
who will shepherd my people Israel.'

Then Herod summoned the wise men to see him privately. He asked them the exact date on which the star had appeared, and sent them on to Bethlehem. 'Go and find out all about the child,' he said 'and when you have found him, let me know, so that I too may go and do him homage.' Having listened to what the king had to say, they set out. And there in front of them was the star they had seen rising; it went forward and halted over the place where the child was. The sight of the star filled them with delight, and going into the house they saw the child with his mother Mary, and falling to their knees they did him homage. Then, opening their treasures, they offered him gifts of gold and frankincense and myrrh. But they were warned in a dream not to go back to Herod, and returned to their own country by a different way.

Wise Men from the East

The Wise Men, with their clever knowledge of astronomy and their lavish gifts, represent all that is best in worldly values. They also have a bit of magic about them, for frankincense and myrrh were used in spells, and the word for 'wise men' can also mean 'magicians'. They have real wisdom and its reward, and yet they lay it all at Jesus's feet. It might be worth asking at this beginning of the year whether we submit all our skills and comforts to Jesus. It is not humility - just a true scale of values.

The story also rests on the sharp contrast between King Herod and the Wise Men. Herod was a Jew, so he should have recognised and honoured the Jewish Messiah. Not at all! He tries to kill the Messiah. By contrast, the Wise Men, arriving from the equivalent of Outer Space, carry on their search till they find Jesus and humbly bow before him. This poses a nasty question: we Christians have all the guidance and encouragement of the Church, but how often we find those outside the Church, not even professed Christians, behaving in a more Christian way than we do ourselves?

Question: What skill can I submit to Jesus today?

Seeing Jesus coming towards him, John said, 'Look, there is the lamb of God that takes away the sin of the world. This is the one I spoke of when I said: A man is coming after me who ranks before me because he existed before me. I did not know him myself, and yet it was to reveal him to Israel that I came baptising with water.' John also declared, 'I saw the Spirit coming down on him from heaven like a dove and resting on him. I did not know him myself, but he who sent me to baptise with water had said to me, "The man on whom you see the Spirit come down and rest is the one who is going to baptise with the Holy Spirit." Yes, I have seen and I am the witness that he is the Chosen One of God.'

The Lamb of God

By contrast to the other Gospels, where the reader observes the disciples discovering gradually who Jesus is, John gives us a week between the Baptism and the Marriage Feast of Cana, during which Jesus is given increasingly significant titles by those who meet him: Rabbi, the Messiah, Son of God, King of Israel. Perhaps the most significant of all are those given by the Baptist himself: Lamb of God and Chosen One of God. Lamb of God overarches the Gospel, for it comes again at the Crucifixion. According to John Jesus dies at the moment the paschal lambs were being slaughtered in the Temple, and John alone refers to Jesus the scriptural saying: 'Not one bone of his will be broken' (*Jn* 19:36), originally part of the instructions for the sacrificing of the lamb at the Festival of Passover (*Ex* 12:46). In the Book of Revelation Jesus is represented standing 'as a Lamb that seemed to have been sacrificed'. It is therefore an image both of his suffering and of his triumph. It links up with the picture of Jesus as the Suffering Servant of the Lord who moves through suffering and humiliation to vindication and to the triumph of God.

Reflection: Reflect on Jesus as the Lamb standing as though sacrificed.

Hearing that John had been arrested Jesus went back to Galilee, and leaving Nazareth he went and settled in Capernaum, a lakeside town on the borders of Zebulun and Naphtali. In this way the prophecy of Isaiah was to be fulfilled:

> Land of Zebulun! Land of Naphtali!
> Way of the sea on the far side of Jordan,
> Galilee of the nations!
> The people that lived in darkness
> has seen a great light;
> on those who dwell in the land and shadow of death
> a light has dawned.

From that moment Jesus began his preaching with the message, 'Repent, for the kingdom of heaven is close at hand'.

As he was walking by the Sea of Galilee he saw two brothers, Simon, who was called Peter, and his brother Andrew; they were making a cast in the lake with their net, for they were fishermen. And he said to them, 'Follow me and I will make you fishers of men.' And they left their nets at once and followed him.

Going on from there he saw another pair of brothers, James son of Zebedee and his brother John; they were in their boat with their father Zebedee, mending their nets, and he called them. At once, leaving the boat and their father, they followed him.

He went round the whole of Galilee teaching in their synagogues, proclaiming the Good News of the kingdom and curing all kinds of diseases and sickness among the people.

The Call of the First Disciples

This is the beginning of Jesus's ministry. Matthew first introduces us to Galilee, characteristically quoting the scriptures to show that they are being fulfilled, and in what way. Galilee is called 'Galilee of the gentiles' only in this passage, and it was not a particularly notable feature of Galilee. Archaeology shows that Jewish observance was strong in the region. Contemporary literature shows that there was a lively tradition of prayerful charismatic rabbis with a warm devotion to the Lord. Jesus begins his ministry by proclaiming the imminence of the Kingdom of God, which will be the subject of all his activity. Then he begins to form the new Israel by calling his team together. The Christian imagination tends to combine this scene with the scene with the Baptist in the Jordan Valley in the Gospel of John, which gives at least Peter and Andrew some knowledge of Jesus. But today's narrative must be heard on its own, and the staggering factor is that this is the first time at any rate the sons of Zebedee have set eyes on Jesus. As he passes by he calls them, and such is the electrifying power of his charismatic personality that they simply drop everything and follow this total stranger - immediately, as the evangelist stresses each time.

Question: Do I ever follow Jesus's call immediately and unconditionally?

Seeing the crowds, Jesus went up the hill. There he sat down and was joined by his disciples. Then he began to speak. This is what he taught them:

'How happy are the poor in spirit:
theirs is the kingdom of heaven.
Happy the gentle:
they shall have the earth for their heritage.
Happy those who mourn:
they shall be comforted.
Happy those who hunger and thirst for what
   is right:
they shall be satisfied.
Happy the merciful:
they shall have mercy shown them.
Happy the pure in heart:
they shall see God.
Happy the peacemakers:
they shall be called sons of God.
Happy those who are persecuted in the cause
   of right:
theirs is the kingdom of heaven.

'Happy are you when people abuse you and persecute you and speak all kinds of calumny against you on my account. Rejoice and be glad, for your reward will be great in heaven.'

The Beatitudes

These eight blessings stand at the head of the Sermon on the Mount, pointing out eight ways in which we can welcome God into our lives. They are ways of living out God's blessing. The first and the last knit them all together with 'theirs is the Kingdom of Heaven'. Luke also begins his Sermon on the Plain with four such blessings - only his blessings are more on those who are materially poor and in need, whereas Matthew's concentrate on the spiritual attitudes required of the Christian, 'poor *in spirit*, hunger and thirst *for justice*'. Jesus came to proclaim the Kingship of his Father, and these are ways of living it. For each of them, do you know someone who exemplifies the attitude? Which is your own favourite? For most of them there are Gospel incidents in which Jesus sums them up, like the entry into Jerusalem on a donkey as the gentle King, or the love he shows in his welcome to sinners, or his bringing peace to those tortured by disease or contempt, or his purity of heart in his single-minded pre-occupation with his Father's will, and finally his acceptance of persecution for what he knew to be right.

Question: Are any of these qualities more basic than others?

Jesus said to his disciples: 'You are the salt of the earth. But if salt becomes tasteless, what can make it salty again? It is good for nothing, and can only be thrown out to be trampled underfoot by men.

'You are the light of the world. A city built on a hill-top cannot be hidden. No one lights a lamp to put it under a tub; they put it on the lamp-stand where it shines for everyone in the house. In the same way your light must shine in the sight of men, so that, seeing your good works, they may give the praise to your Father in heaven.'

Salt and Light

Matthew here takes two piquant images from the words of Jesus which he found in Mark's Gospel and builds them up. Immediately after the Beatitudes, with which he began the Sermon on the Mount, he shows that these Christian attitudes are not just for our own benefit, but are to change the world. The first is a warning, the second a promise. Christians are to be salt for the whole world. Imagine a perpetual diet of food without any tang or taste, soggy and insipid! This would be the world if Christians did not spread the message of Christ, did not impart to the world the flavour brought by Christ's message. What would the world be without that message and challenge of the generosity and salvation of Christ which we profess? Yes, of course much of the same message may come to the world through other great world faiths, but the full challenge and the full promise is in Christ. The same is true for the second image, that of light. Imagine a world of darkness, where we had to feel our way and are never quite sure of shapes and purposes! And then what a difference occurs when the sun rises over the horizon or the light is switched on. Such is the difference which Christianity - and our Christianity - must make to the world.

Question: How should the Christian set out to be salt and light to today's world?

Jesus said to his disciples: 'For I tell you, if your virtue goes no deeper than that of the scribes and Pharisees, you will never get into the kingdom of heaven.

'You have learnt how it was said to our ancestors: You must not kill; and if anyone does kill he must answer for it before the court. But I say this to you: anyone who is angry with his brother will answer for it before the court.

'You have learnt how it was said: You must not commit adultery. But I say this to you: if a man looks at a woman lustfully, he has already committed adultery with her in his heart.

'Again, you have learnt how it was said to our ancestors: You must not break your oath, but must fulfil your oaths to the Lord. But I say this to you: do not swear at all. All you need say is "Yes" if you mean yes, "No" if you mean no; anything more than this comes from the evil one.'

Jesus the Law

Jesus is the completion of the Law of God, given to Israel through Moses. He has come not to sweep it away, but to perfect it. In this part of the Sermon on the Mount Matthew has gathered together six instances (four this week, two next Sunday) of the ways in which Jesus brings the Law to perfection. The first factor to notice, however, is that Jesus does not hesitate to adjust the divine Law on his own authority, for he too has divine authority. Each correction begins with a statement of the old Law and boldly goes on, 'But I say this to you...'

Each of the corrections has its own character. The first is about enmity, the sixth about love. About enmity, it is not enough merely to forego violent injury; we must even expel enmity from our hearts, positively seeking reconciliation, whether the offence is our fault or not. About lust, it is similarly not enough to forego acts of lust; we must not even harbour such thoughts in our hearts. About divorce, the easy toleration of divorce in the Jewish Law is swept away, and Jesus uncompromisingly calls it fornication. About truth, it is not enough to keep a legal oath; we must be people whose every word can be relied upon. These are Jesus's demanding standards.

Question: Which is the most difficult of these demands?

(Longer form Matthew 5:17-37)

Jesus said to his disciples: 'You have learnt how it was said: Eye for eye and tooth for tooth. But I say this to you: offer the wicked man no resistance. On the contrary, if anyone hits you on the right cheek, offer him the other as well; if a man takes you to law and would have your tunic, let him have your cloak as well. And if anyone orders you to go one mile, go two miles with him. Give to anyone who asks, and if anyone wants to borrow, do not turn away.

'You have learnt how it was said: You must love your neighbour and hate your enemy. But I say this to you: love your enemies and pray for those who persecute you; in this way you will be sons of your Father in heaven, for he causes his sun to rise on bad men as well as good, and his rain to fall on honest and dishonest men alike. For if you love those who love you, what right have you to claim any credit? Even the tax collectors do as much, do they not? And if you save your greetings for your brothers, are you doing anything exceptional? Even the pagans do as much, do they not? You must therefore be perfect just as your heavenly Father is perfect.'

Jesus the Law

Following on from the four adjustments of the Law in last Sunday's Gospel come two more, perhaps the most demanding. The Law of Moses had limited revenge: only a tooth might be taken for a tooth, only an eye for an eye, not life itself. Jesus, however, will not tolerate even this limited vengeance; he allows no revenge at all. Again and again in the course of the Gospel Jesus returns to this need for unconditional forgiveness. We daringly engage ourselves to it whenever we say the Lord's Prayer: 'forgive us just as we forgive...'

The final demand, however, is the most challenging of all. There is in fact no passage of the canonical Scripture which encourages 'hate your enemy'. In any case, just as God lavishes his benefits of life, sun and rain on good and evil alike, so we must put no limits to our love. Only in this way - think of the first reading! - can we attempt to honour and imitate the holiness of God. This is what it means to be a son of God, 'sons of your Father in heaven': only by following in his way and by fulfilling his designs can we be integrated into his family. There can be no enmity in Christianity.

Question: Can I really forgive with no trace of animosity?

Jesus said to his disciples: 'No one can be the slave of two masters: he will either hate the first and love the second, or treat the first with respect and the second with scorn. You cannot be the slave both of God and of money.

'That is why I am telling you not to worry about your life and what you are to eat, nor about your body and how you are to clothe it. Surely life means more than food, and the body more than clothing! Look at the birds in the sky. They do not sow or reap or gather into barns; yet your heavenly Father feeds them. Are you not worth much more than they are? Can any of you, for all his worrying, add one single cubit to his span of life? And why worry about clothing? Think of the flowers growing in the fields; they never have to work or spin; yet I assure you that not even Solomon in all his regalia was robed like one of these. Now if that is how God clothes the grass in the field which is there today and thrown into the furnace tomorrow, will he not much more look after you, you men of little faith? So do not worry; do not say, "What are we to eat? What are we to drink? How are we to be clothed?" It is the pagans who set their hearts on all these things. Your heavenly Father knows you need them all. Set your hearts on his kingdom first, and on his righteousness, and all these other things will be given you as well. So do not worry about tomorrow; tomorrow will take care of itself. Each day has enough trouble of its own.'

Trust in God's Care

At the beginning of this passage we are told that you cannot serve two masters, a lesson which in the Gospel of Luke is illustrated by the parable of the Crafty Steward. Unscrupulously, when he receives notice to quit, he defrauds his master by cutting down the sums owed by his master's debtors, and so wins their friendship which will continue to support him. *(Lk 16:1-13)*. In Matthew's Sermon on the Mount this whole passage, promising God's care for his faithful, comes after the requirement that we should serve God 'in secret', not blazoning our good works before onlookers. That passage is omitted from the semi-continuous reading of the Sermon because it is used at the beginning of Lent, on Ash Wednesday, so here we go straight on to the promise of a reward for faithful service. It is a commonplace of philosophers that no amount of worrying will increase our safety or comfort, but we need Christian faith to find our satisfaction and security in the divine protection. God's loving, maternal care does not preclude prolonged suffering, leading St Teresa of Avila to exclaim to Jesus: 'If you treat your friends like this, it is no wonder that you have so few of them.'

Question: Is it really possible to serve two masters, fairly and satisfactorily?

Jesus was led by the Spirit out into the wilderness to be tempted by the devil. He fasted for forty days and forty nights, after which he was very hungry, and the tempter came and said to him, 'If you are the Son of God, tell these stones to turn into loaves.' But he replied, 'Scripture says:

> Man does not live on bread alone
> but on every word that comes from the mouth of God.'

The devil then took him to the holy city and made him stand on the parapet of the Temple. 'If you are the Son of God' he said 'throw yourself down; for scripture says:

> He will put you in his angels' charge,
> and they will support you on their hands
> in case you hurt your foot against a stone.'

Jesus said to him, 'Scripture also says:

> You must not put the Lord your God to the test.'

Next, taking him to a very high mountain, the devil showed him all the kingdoms of the world and their splendour. 'I will give you all these' he said, 'if you fall at my feet and worship me.' Then Jesus replied, 'Be off, Satan! For scripture says:

> You must worship the Lord your God,
> and serve him alone.'

Then the devil left him, and angels appeared and looked after him.

The Testing of Jesus

By putting this scene of the testing of Jesus at the beginning of Lent, the Church shows that it sees Lent as a period of testing. Matthew sees this moment as the testing of God's Son, just as the People of God Israel - God's son, whom he brought out of Egypt into the desert - was tested for forty years. We may also see it as the time when Jesus reflected on the mode of his mission. His mission was to bring the Kingship of God to a new realisation: how should he do this? The Tempter suggests false ways, which Jesus rejects, one after another, each time with a word from Scripture, the Word of God. He rejects the idea of the Messiah merely producing the luxury of the plenteous messianic banquet (stones into food). He rejects the idea of a startling personal miracle which none could gainsay (the leap from the Temple). He rejects the suggestion of entering into league with the Tempter's own values of pride and dominion (rule over the world). At the same time Jesus shows himself to be the Second Moses, the founder of a new People of God: like Moses, he spends forty days and forty nights fasting; like Moses he is taken up on to a high mountain, from where he can see not merely all the territory of the Holy Land, but all the kingdoms of the earth.

Question: What is the chief fault which tempts the Church away from the way of Christ today?

Jesus took with him Peter and James and his brother John and led them up a high mountain where they could be alone. There in their presence he was transfigured; his face shone like the sun and his clothes became as white as the light. Suddenly Moses and Elijah appeared to them; they were talking with him. Then Peter spoke to Jesus. 'Lord,' he said 'it is wonderful for us to be here; if you wish, I will make three tents here, one for you, one for Moses and one for Elijah.' He was still speaking when suddenly a bright cloud covered them with shadow, and from the cloud there came a voice which said, 'This is my Son, the Beloved; he enjoys my favour. Listen to him.' When they heard this, the disciples fell on their faces, overcome with fear. But Jesus came up and touched them. 'Stand up,' he said 'do not be afraid.' And when they raised their eyes they saw no one but only Jesus.

As they came down from the mountain Jesus gave them this order. 'Tell no one about the vision until the Son of Man has risen from the dead.'

The Transfiguration

Each year on this second Sunday of Lent we read the account of the Transfiguration. It was the moment when the disciples were shown the divinity of Jesus on the Holy Mountain. The scene is reminiscent of Moses's encounter with God on Sinai, when his face, too, shone like the sun. Moses and Elijah are present because they are the two Old Testament figures who experienced the presence of God on the Holy Mountain. With his usual impetuous generosity Peter attempts to 'freeze' the moment. The public declaration of Jesus as God's Son at the Baptism is repeated, but with the addition that Jesus is the authorised divine teacher; Matthew is alert to the implications for the Church of the presence of Christ as teacher. The cloud is also a symbol of God's presence, to which the human response only can be to fall to the ground in fear and reverence. The awesome moment of revelation cannot, however, last, and Jesus brings his disciples back to the dire realities before them with the reminder that his death must precede the revelation of his glory at the Resurrection. Until they have experienced the limitless generosity of his death, and the vindication by God of this love, they are not ready to spread the message of Jesus.

Question: Why are the disciples forbidden to spread the message till after the Resurrection?

Jesus came to the Samaritan town called Sychar, near the land that Jacob gave to his son Joseph. Jacob's well is there and Jesus, tired by the journey, sat straight down by the well. It was about the sixth hour. When a Samaritan woman came to draw water, Jesus said to her, 'Give me a drink.' His disciples had gone into the town to buy food. The Samaritan woman said to him, 'What? You are a Jew and you ask me, a Samaritan for a drink?' – Jews in fact, do not associate with Samaritans. Jesus replied:

> 'If you only knew what God is offering
> and who it is that is saying to you:
> Give me a drink,
> you would have been the one to ask,
> and he would have given you living water.'

'You have no bucket, sir,' she answered, 'and the well is deep: how could you get this living water? Are you a greater man than our father Jacob who gave us this well and drank from it himself with his sons and his cattle?' Jesus replied:

> 'Whoever drinks this water
> will get thirsty again;
> but anyone who drinks the water that I shall give
> will never be thirsty again:
> the water that I shall give
> will turn into a spring inside him, welling up
>   to eternal life.'

'Sir,' said the woman, 'give me some of that water, so that I may never get thirsty and never have to come here again to draw water.'

'I see you are a prophet, sir' said the woman. 'Our fathers worshipped on this mountain, while you say that Jerusalem is the place where one ought to worship.' Jesus said:

> 'Believe me, woman, the hour is coming
> when you will worship the Father
> neither on this mountain nor in Jerusalem.
> You worship what you do not know;
> we worship what we do know;
> for salvation comes from the Jews.
> But the hour will come – in fact it is here already –
> when true worshippers will worship the Father in
> spirit and truth:
> that is the kind of worshipper
> the Father wants.
> God is spirit,
> and those who worship
> must worship in spirit and truth.'

The woman said to him, 'I know that Messiah – that is, Christ – is coming; and when he comes he will tell us everything.' 'I who am speaking to you,' said Jesus 'I am he.'

Many Samaritans of that town had believed in him on the strength of the woman's testimony when she said, 'He told me all I have ever done,' so, when the Samaritans came up to him, they begged him to stay with them. He stayed for two days, and when he spoke to them many more came to believe; and they said to the woman, 'Now we no longer believe because of what you told us; we have heard him ourselves and we know that he really is the saviour of the world.'

Разговорот со Самарјанката

THIRD SUNDAY OF LENT

The Samaritan at the Well

In this lively dialogue Jesus almost seems to be teasing the Samaritan woman, deliberately leading her into misunderstanding about what he means by living water or about the conditions of worship. Undaunted, she gives as good as she gets, replying with a cheeky series of sarcastic questions, gradually edging nearer to the truth: an open-minded Jew - greater than our father Jacob, a prophet, and finally acknowledging him as the Messiah. With its serious message it is a lovely example of Jesus's willingness to engage with people as they are, and of his openness with women.

On these last three Sundays of Lent before Palm Sunday in Cycle A, the Church lays before us the three great symbols of the Baptisms which will be celebrated at Easter. This concerns not only those who will be baptised at the Easter Vigil, but all those who are invited to renew our baptismal promise and commitment at Easter. Then we enter afresh into the living and nourishing water of God's love which surpasses any food or drink, into the light which enlightens the blind (the Cure of the Man Born Blind) and true life (the Raising of Lazarus).

Question: In prayer, should we treat Jesus as the Samaritan Woman does?

(Longer form John 4:5-42)

As Jesus went along, he saw a man who had been blind from birth. He spat on the ground, made a paste with the spittle, put this over the eyes of the blind man and said to him, 'Go and wash in the Pool of Siloam' (a name that means 'sent'). So the blind man went off and washed himself, and came away with his sight restored.

His neighbours and people who earlier had seen him begging said, 'Isn't this the man who used to sit and beg?' Some said, 'Yes, it is the same one.' Others said, 'No, he only looks like him.' The man himself said, 'I am the man.'

They brought the man who had been blind to the Pharisees. It had been a sabbath day when Jesus made the paste and opened the man's eyes, so when the Pharisees asked him how he had come to see, he said, 'He put a paste on my eyes, and I washed, and I can see.' Then some of the Pharisees said, 'This man cannot be from God: he does not keep the sabbath.' Others said, 'How could a sinner produce signs like this?' And there was disagreement among them. So they spoke to the blind man again, 'What have you to say about him yourself, now that he has opened your eyes?' 'He is a prophet' replied the man.

'Are you trying to teach us,' they replied 'and you a sinner through and through, since you were born!' And they drove him away.

Jesus heard they had driven him away, and when he found him he said to him, 'Do you believe in the Son of Man?' 'Sir,' the man replied 'tell me who he is so that I may believe in him.' Jesus said, 'You are looking at him; he is speaking to you.' The man said, 'Lord, I believe', and worshipped him.

The Cure of the Blind Man

The second of the three great Johannine readings about water, light and life featured in the Baptisms of Easter gives us the splendid account of Jesus bringing light to the blind man in the Temple. It is full of Johannine contrasts and irony. The 'Jews' or the Pharisees think they have the light and knowledge, but the more they abuse the man born blind, the clearer their own darkness and ignorance become. The more they try to thrust him away from Jesus, the more they push him into seeking refuge in him. Much of the colouring of the scene comes from the controversies towards the end of the first century, when the Pharisees were the only branch of Judaism to survive after the destruction of Jerusalem by the Romans. The New Testament shows that there was bitter opposition between those Jews who accepted the divine claims for Jesus, and those who rejected them. This is especially clear in the fear of the blind man's parents that they would be excluded from the synagogue if they accepted that Jesus's grant of sight was a sign of his divine mission. The doughty and pugnacious man born blind has no such hesitation!

Question: Where did these opponents of Jesus go wrong?

(Longer form John 9:1-41)

The sisters sent this message to Jesus, 'Lord, the man you love is ill.' On receiving the message, Jesus said, 'This sickness will end not in death but in God's glory, and through it the Son of God will be glorified.'

Jesus loved Martha and her sister and Lazarus, yet when he heard that Lazarus was ill he stayed where he was for two more days before saying to the disciples, 'Let us go to Judaea.'

On arriving, Jesus found that Lazarus had been in the tomb for four days already. When Martha heard that Jesus had come she went to meet him. Mary remained sitting in the house. Martha said to Jesus, 'If you had been here, my brother would not have died, but I know that, even now, whatever you ask of God, he will grant you.' 'Your brother' said Jesus to her 'will rise again.' Martha said, 'I know he will rise again at the resurrection on the last day.' Jesus said:

'I am the resurrection and the life.

If anyone believes in me, even though he dies
   he will live,
and whoever lives and believes in me
will never die.

Do you believe this?'

'Yes Lord,' she said 'I believe that you are the Christ, the Son of God, the one who was to come into this world.

Jesus said in great distress, with a sigh that came straight from the heart, 'Where have you put him?' They said, 'Lord, come and see.' Jesus wept; and the Jews said, 'See how much he loved him!' But there were some who remarked, 'He opened the eyes of the blind man, could he not have prevented this man's death?' Still sighing, Jesus reached the tomb: it was a cave with a stone to close the opening. Jesus said, 'Take the stone away.' Martha said to him, 'Lord, by now he will smell; this is the fourth day.' Jesus replied, 'Have I not told you that if you believe you will see the glory of God?' So they took away the stone. Then Jesus lifted up his eyes and said:

'Father, I thank you for hearing my prayer.
I knew indeed that you always hear me,
but I speak
for the sake of all these who stand round me,
so that they may believe it was you who sent me.'

When he had said this, he cried in a loud voice, 'Lazarus, here! Come out!' The dead man came out, his feet and hands bound with bands of stuff and a cloth round his face. Jesus said to them, 'Unbind him, let him go free.'

Many of the Jews who had come to visit Mary and had seen what he did believed in him.

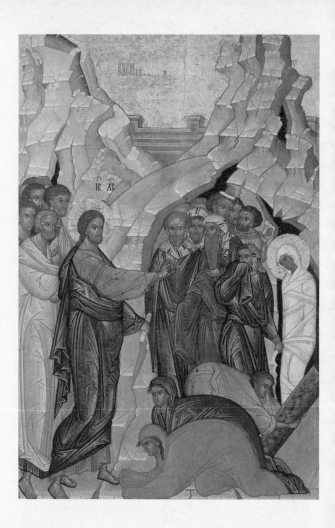

The Raising of Lazarus

The third of these great Johannine Gospel readings on the Sundays of Lent, leading up to and preparing us for the Baptisms of the new members of Christ at the Easter Vigil, grips us with the story of Jesus's gift of life to his friend Lazarus. This is not the same as the gift of life to us by Jesus in the Resurrection, for Lazarus returns to ordinary human life, and will die again, whereas the Christian resurrection transforms us into a new way of life, giving us a life which is a participation in the divine life. But the resurrection of Lazarus is the last and greatest of Jesus's signs, his marvellous works which point towards and hint at this final gift of divine life. The first of the signs was the transformation of the water of the Law into the wine of the messianic wedding banquet at Cana. These signs show who Jesus really is. As well as showing the divine power of Jesus - for only God can give life - they also show the real, human love of Jesus for his friends. He is upset by Lazarus's death and weeps for him, sharing the human sorrow of his family as he shares our sorrows too.

Question: Is death something to fear?

(Longer form John 11:1-45)

The Passion of Our Lord Jesus Christ
According to Matthew

The symbols in the following passion narrative represent:

N **Narrator**   J **Jesus**   O **Other single speaker**
C **Crowd, or more than one speaker**

N Jesus, then, was brought before the governor, and the governor put to him this question:

O Are you the king of the Jews?

N Jesus replied:

J It is you who say it.

N But when he was accused by the chief priests and the elders he refused to answer at all. Pilate then said to him:

O Do you not hear how many charges they have brought against you?

N But to the governor's complete amazement, he offered no reply to any of the charges.

At festival time it was the governor's practice to release a prisoner for the people, anyone they chose. Now there was at that time a notorious prisoner whose name was Barabbas. So when the crowd gathered, Pilate said to them,

O Which do you want me to release for you: Barabbas or Jesus who is called Christ?

N For Pilate knew it was out of jealousy that they had handed him over.

Now as he was seated in the chair of judgement, his wife sent him a message,

O Have nothing to do with that man; I have been upset all day by a dream I had about him.

N The chief priests and the elders, however, had persuaded the crowd to demand the release of Barabbas and the execution of Jesus. So when the governor spoke and asked them:

O Which of the two do you want me to release for you?

N They said:

C Barabbas.

N Pilate said to them:

O What am I to do with Jesus who is called Christ?

N They all said:

C Let him be crucified!

N Pilate asked:

O Why? What harm has he done?

N But they shouted all the louder,

C Let him be crucified!

N Then Pilate saw that he was making no impression, that in fact a riot was imminent. So he took some water, washed his hands in front of the crowd and said:

O I am innocent of this man's blood. It is your concern.

N And the people, to a man, shouted back:

C His blood be on us and on our children!

N Then he released Barabbas for them. He ordered Jesus to be first scourged and then handed over to be crucified.

The governor's soldiers took Jesus with them into the Praetorium and collected the whole cohort round him. Then they stripped him and made him wear a scarlet cloak, and having twisted some thorns into a crown they put this on his head and placed a reed in his right hand. To make fun of him they knelt to him saying:

C Hail, king of the Jews!

N And they spat on him and took the reed and struck him on the head with it. And when they had finished making fun of him, they took off the cloak and dressed him in his own clothes and led him away to crucify him.

On their way out, they came across a man from Cyrene, Simon by name, and enlisted him to carry his cross. When they had reached a place called Golgotha, that is, the place of the skull, they gave him wine to drink. When they had finished crucifying him they shared out his clothing by casting lots, and then sat down and stayed there keeping guard over him. Above his head was placed the charge against him; it read: 'This is Jesus, the King of the Jews.' At the same time two robbers were crucified with him, one on the right and one on the left.

The passers-by jeered at him; they shook their heads and said:

C So you would destroy the Temple and rebuild it in three days! Then save yourself! If you are God's son, come down from the cross!

N The chief priests with the scribes and elders mocked him in the same way, saying:

C He saved others; he cannot save himself. He is the King of Israel; let him come down from the cross now, and we will believe in him. He put his trust in God; now let God rescue him if he wants him. For he did say, 'I am the son of God.'

N Even the robbers who were crucified with him taunted him in the same way.

From the sixth hour there was darkness over all the land until the ninth hour. And about the ninth hour, Jesus cried out in a loud voice:

J Eli, Eli, lama sabachthani?

N That is: 'My God, my God, why have you deserted me?' When some of those who stood there heard this, they said:

C The man is calling on Elijah,

N and one of them quickly ran to get a sponge which he dipped in vinegar and, putting it on a reed, gave it him to drink. The rest of them said:

C Wait! See if Elijah will come to save him.

N But Jesus, again crying out in a loud voice, yielded up his spirit.

All kneel and pause a moment.

N At that, the veil of the Temple was torn in two from top to bottom; the earth quaked; the rocks were split; the tombs opened and the bodies of many holy men rose from the dead, and these, after his resurrection, came out of the tombs, entered the Holy City and appeared to a number of people.

Meanwhile the centurion, together with the others guarding Jesus, had seen the earthquake and all that was taking place, and they were terrified and said:

C In truth this was a son of God.

(Longer form Matthew 26:14-27:66)

The Passion of Christ According to Matthew

The accounts of the Passion given by the four evangelists are not identical. The basic outline of these dreadful events was clear enough. It is confirmed by the contemporary Jewish historian Josephus, who tells us that Jesus was crucified by Pontius Pilate at the instigation of the Jewish leaders. The task of the Gospel writers is not to relay to us the raw facts, but to help us understand their significance. Each stresses a particular aspect. For instance, John underlines that this was the triumph of Jesus: he shows his divinity already at the arrest scene. He himself yielded up his Spirit only when he had completed his task. Matthew's pre-occupation with Judaism dictates that he show in detail how the events accord with God's plan revealed in the scriptures. Almost every incident is told in such a way that hearers familiar with the scriptures would catch allusions to the biblical writings: nowhere is this more obvious than in the account of the death of Judas. Though Pilate the governor must bear the final responsibility, Matthew also stresses the pressure put on him by the crowd manipulated by the politically adept Jewish authorities, culminating in the horrific cry: 'His blood be on us and on our children' - an allusion to the sufferings undergone by the next generation during the siege of Jerusalem by the Romans. The significance of the events is further underlined by the apocalyptic earthquake at Jesus's death, and by the immediate release of the blessed dead, who come at last into the Holy City.

It was very early on the first day of the week and still dark, when Mary of Magdala came to the tomb. She saw that the stone had been moved away from the tomb and came running to Simon Peter and the other disciple, the one Jesus loved. 'They have taken the Lord out of the tomb' she said 'and we don't know where they have put him.'

So Peter set out with the other disciple to go to the tomb. They ran together, but the other disciple, running faster than Peter, reached the tomb first; he bent down and saw the linen cloths lying on the ground, but did not go in. Simon Peter who was following now came up, went right into the tomb, saw the linen cloths on the ground, and also the cloth that had been over his head; this was not with the linen cloths but rolled up in a place by itself. Then the other disciple who had reached the tomb first also went in; he saw and he believed. Till this moment they had failed to understand the teaching of scripture, that he must rise from the dead.

The Empty Tomb

There are several accounts in the various Gospels of the discovery of the empty tomb. The slight variations between them show all the marks of oral tradition, for in genuine oral tradition each 'performance' is different. Different people tell the story slightly differently, stressing different aspects. This story stresses the proof that the tomb really was empty, for the apostles examine the evidence carefully. Other accounts concentrate less on the evidence and more on the message, that they will meet the Risen Lord in Galilee. It was important to establish that the tomb was empty, to prevent the charge that the meetings with the Risen Christ were simply ghost appearances. Apart from the proof that this was a real, living and bodily person, these meetings stress two factors, the power of the Risen Christ and the commission given to the disciples. They are to go out into the whole world and spread the message, always accompanied by and strengthened by Christ himself. In this account Simon Peter is clearly the senior, authority figure, to whom the beloved disciple defers. But it is the love of the beloved disciple which immediately brings him to faith.

Question: Is the empty tomb the chief evidence for the Resurrection?

In the evening of that same day, the first day of the week, the doors were closed in the room where the disciples were, for fear of the Jews. Jesus came and stood among them. He said to them, 'Peace be with you,' and showed them his hands and his side. The disciples were filled with joy when they saw the Lord, and he said to them again,'Peace be with you. As the Father sent me, so am I sending you.'

After saying this he breathed on them and said: 'Receive the Holy Spirit. For those whose sins you forgive, they are forgiven; for those whose sins you retain, they are retained.'

Thomas, called the Twin, who was one of the Twelve, was not with them when Jesus came. When the disciples said, 'We have seen the Lord,' he answered, 'Unless I see the holes that the nails made in his hands and can put my finger into the holes they made, and unless I can put my hand into his side, I refuse to believe.' Eight days later the disciples were in the house again and Thomas was with them. The doors were closed, but Jesus came in and stood among them. 'Peace be with you,' he said. Then he spoke to Thomas, 'Put your finger here; look, here are my hands. Give me your hand; put it into my side. Doubt no longer but believe.' Thomas replied, 'My Lord and my God!'

Jesus said to him: 'You believe because you can see me. Happy are those who have not seen and yet believe.'

There were many other signs that Jesus worked and the disciples saw, but they are not recorded in this book. These are recorded so that you may believe that Jesus is the Christ, the Son of God, and that believing this you may have life through his name.

The Peace of the Risen Christ

This passage from John's Gospel has all the more significance because it brings the Gospel to a close. The story of the breakfast party with the Risen Christ on the shore of the Lake of Galilee is a sort of appendix. The storyline of the main Gospel ends with Thomas blurting out: 'My Lord and my God'. The Gospel therefore ends, as it began with the only two unmistakable declarations in the New Testament of the divinity of Jesus. 'The Word was God' and 'My Lord and my God' bracket the Gospel, showing the purpose and angle of the whole, to show that Jesus is God. It complements the other Gospels: they show a man who is also God, whereas this Gospel shows a God who is also man. It is with the divine authority that Jesus confers on his Church the divine power to forgive. Real forgiveness is indeed Godlike. It is not simply 'forgive and forget', but forgiveness in the knowledge that a hurt has occurred. Just as a bone, broken and merged together again, can be stronger than it was before it was broken, so forgiveness can create a real link of love on both sides, a treasured secret of divine graciousness between forgiver and forgiven.

Question: Am I part of the Church's divine power to forgive?

Two of the disciples of Jesus were on their way to a village called Emmaus, seven miles from Jerusalem, and they were talking together about all that had happened. Now as they talked this over, Jesus himself came up and walked by their side; but something prevented them from recognising him. He said to them, 'What matters are you discussing as you walk along?' They stopped short, their faces downcast.

Then one of them, called Cleopas, answered him, 'You must be the only person staying in Jerusalem who does not know the things that have been happening there these last few days.' 'What things?' he asked. 'All about Jesus of Nazareth' they answered 'who proved he was a great prophet by the things he said and did in the sight of God and of the whole people; and how our chief priests and our leaders handed him over to be sentenced to death, and had him crucified. Our own hope had been that he would be the one to set Israel free. And this is not all: two whole days have gone by since it all happened; and some women from our group have astounded us: they went to the tomb in the early morning, and when they did not find the body, they came back to tell us they had seen a vision of angels who declared he was alive. Some of our friends went to the tomb and found everything exactly as the women had reported, but of him they saw nothing.'

Then he said to them, 'You foolish men! So slow to believe the full message of the prophets! Was it not ordained that the Christ should suffer and so enter into his glory?' Then, starting with Moses and going through all the prophets, he explained to them the passages throughout the scriptures that were about himself.

When they drew near to the village to which they were going, he made as if to go on; but they pressed him to stay with them. 'It is nearly evening' they said 'and the day is almost over.' So he went in to stay with them. Now while he was with them at table, he took the bread and said the blessing; then he broke it and handed it to them. And their eyes were opened and they recognised him; but he had vanished from their sight. Then they said to each other, 'Did not our hearts burn within us as he talked to us on the road and explained the scriptures to us?'

They set out that instant and returned to Jerusalem. There they found the Eleven assembled together with their companions, who said to them, 'Yes, it is true. The Lord has risen and has appeared to Simon.' Then they told their story of what had happened on the road and how they had recognised him at the breaking of bread.

The Journey to Emmaus

This attractive and delicate story is the story of the journey to faith in the Risen Christ: it occurs in any Christian instruction, and especially in the Eucharist, formed from instruction based on the scriptures, and then brought to its fulfilment in the Sacrament. The two disciples (are they man and woman, as so often in Luke, perhaps Cleopas and his wife?) start off deep in depression and disappointment. But they are open minded and willing to learn as the Stranger explains to them from Scripture the meaning of events. Their hearts burn within them at the Stranger's words, but their eyes remain closed. It is only in the sacramental meal that they recognise the Risen Christ. This is the story of any Christian instruction, culminating in the Eucharist, for the Eucharist is a Sacrament of Initiation, bringing us to the intimate, personal encounter with Christ. Once they have been enlightened and have learnt the profound meaning of the events, the truth of the scriptures and the Resurrection, then the disciples return to the Holy City and carry on their own Christian apostolate by spreading the news of the Resurrection. This is the shape of the Christian vocation which we all receive, to assimilate and pass on the meaning of Christ's Resurrection.

Question: Is the Old Testament a book for Christians?

Jesus said: 'I tell you most solemnly, anyone who does not enter the sheepfold through the gate, but gets in some other way is a thief and a brigand. The one who enters through the gate is the shepherd of the flock; the gatekeeper lets him in, the sheep hear his voice, one by one he calls his own sheep and leads them out. When he has brought out his flock, he goes ahead of them, and the sheep follow because they know his voice. They never follow a stranger but run away from him: they do not recognise the voice of strangers.'

Jesus told them this parable but they failed to understand what he meant by telling it to them.

So Jesus spoke to them again:

'I tell you most solemnly,
I am the gate of the sheepfold.
All others who have come
are thieves and brigands;
but the sheep took no notice of them.
I am the gate.
Anyone who enters through me will be safe:
he will go freely in and out
and be sure of finding pasture.
The thief comes
only to steal and kill and destroy.
I have come so that they may have life
and have it to the full.'

The Good Shepherd

In each year of the three-year cycle of readings this Sunday is designated Good Shepherd Sunday, with readings from the parable given in John 10. In the first two Sundays after Easter the meetings with the Risen Lord are described, but after that the most important truth about the Risen Lord which the Church puts before us is that Christ is the Good Shepherd. In the Old Testament God is the Shepherd of Israel, and indeed in the neighbouring pastoral nations too, the protective deity of the nation is commonly called their shepherd. As the pastoral ancient world well knew, the duty of the shepherd is to care devotedly for the sheep, with no regard to the personal cost to himself. Ezekiel repeatedly castigates the recent shepherds of Israel for their failure to care for the sheep and for managing the flock for their own personal advantage. It is especially striking that in all four Gospels the divine title of Shepherd is transferred from God to Jesus himself, at least implying not only that Jesus is the perfect shepherd, but also that he is the incarnation of that divine Shepherd, fulfilling the duties which had hitherto been credited to God alone. By his selfless generosity he is the model for all rulers and leaders of nations.

Question: Are you a sheep?

Jesus said to his disciples:

> 'Do not let your hearts be troubled. Trust in God still, and trust in me. There are many rooms in my Father's house; if there were not, I should have told you. I am going now to prepare a place for you, and after I have gone and prepared you a place, I shall return to take you with me; so that where I am you may be too. You know the way to the place where I am going.'

Thomas said, 'Lord, we do not know where you are going, so how can we know the way?' Jesus said:

> 'I am the Way, the Truth and the Life. No one can come to the Father except through me. If you know me, you know my Father too. From this moment you know him and have seen him.'

Philip said, 'Lord, let us see the Father and then we shall be satisfied.' 'Have I been with you all this time, Philip,' said Jesus to him 'and you still do not know me?

> 'To have seen me is to have seen the Father, so how can you say, "Let us see the Father"? Do you not believe that I am in the Father and the Father is in me? The words I say to you I do not speak as from myself: it is the Father, living in me, who is doing this work. You must believe me when I say that I am in the Father and the Father is in me; believe it on the evidence of this work, if for no other reason.
>
> 'I tell you most solemnly, whoever believes in me will perform the same works as I do myself, he will perform even greater works, because I am going to the Father.'

Jesus Warns of his Departure

As the festival of the Ascension approaches Jesus begins to prepare his followers for his own departure from the world. There are two aspects of this. First Jesus speaks of the final purpose, union with the Father, and his preparation of a place for us there. 'There is plenty of room', he says, suggesting not that there are plenty of separate cubicles for different sets of people (bishops, babies, monks and maniacs), but that there is no lack of space. No problem of 'only one wins the prize' in this case. The second aspect is preparation for the future Church on earth, and the almost shocking promise that in the absence of Jesus - but in the strength of his Spirit - his people will do 'even greater works'. Paul teaches that believers 'make up what is lacking in the sufferings of Christ', for in every age the Church fills up the measure of Christ's sufferings; it is a Church which shares its Master's trials. In the same way in every age the Church must carry on the works of Christ. In John the 'works' of Jesus are the marvellous deeds, beyond human powers, which show who Jesus is. We too are called on to perform marvellous deeds, beyond human powers, works of grace and generosity.

Question: In heaven what will our relationship with other people be?

Jesus said to his disciples:

> 'If you love me you will keep my
> commandments.
> I shall ask the Father,
> and he will give you another Advocate
> to be with you for ever,
> that Spirit of truth
> whom the world can never receive
> since it neither sees nor knows him,
> but you know him,
> because he is with you, he is in you.
> I will not leave you orphans;
> I will come back to you.
> In a short time the world will no longer see me;
> but you will see me,
> because I live and you will live.
> On that day
> you will understand that I am in my Father
> and you in me and I in you.
> Anybody who receives my commandments
>   and keeps them
> will be one who loves me;
> and anybody who loves me will be loved
>   by my Father,
> and I shall love him and show myself to him.'

The Advocate whom the Father will Send

Only in John is the Spirit whom the Father will send called 'the Advocate' or 'the Paraclete'. Both names have the same derivation and the same meaning, but the former is from the Latin words, the latter from the Greek. It means someone 'called to one's side' as a helper, principally as a defender in a lawsuit. The word 'Paraclete' also suggests comfort and strength, as implied in the quality *paraclesis* or perseverance. In the discourse after the Last Supper, when Jesus is preparing his disciples for their future task, there are four separate sayings about the Paraclete. The Paraclete is sent both by Jesus and by the Father, but always from the Father's side. The Paraclete, the Spirit of Truth, will teach the disciples everything and lead them into all truth, witnessing to the Father. The Paraclete is 'another Paraclete', that is, other than Jesus, who will make Jesus present when Jesus is no longer physically with them. The close link and interplay between these three figures gives us not only the beginnings of the theology of the Trinity, but also a lasting confidence that Jesus is never absent from his Church. With the guidance and patronage of the Paraclete the Church enters more and more deeply into the understanding of the divine mystery.

Question: Have you ever felt especially helped by the Spirit of Jesus?

The eleven disciples set out for Galilee, to the mountain where Jesus had arranged to meet them. When they saw him they fell down before him, though some hesitated. Jesus came up and spoke to them. He said, 'All authority in heaven and on earth has been given to me. Go, therefore, make disciples of all the nations; baptise them in the name of the Father and of the Son and of the Holy Spirit, and teach them to observe all the commands I gave you. And know that I am with you always; yes, to the end of time.'

A Final Commission to the Disciples

For Matthew this is a momentous climax. Jesus is on the holy mountain. Where is this mountain? We do not know; nor does it matter. The importance is that Jesus is commissioning his followers as the Second Moses. Just as he taught the Sermon on the Mount on the holy mountain, so Moses had given the Old Law on the mount of Sinai. He is the glorious Son of Man of the prophecy of Daniel, to whom all authority on earth was given; but to him is given all authority in heaven and on earth. As Jesus sends them out, he promises that his divine presence will be always with them. It is in the strength of that presence that they will pursue their task. This promise provides the final bracket of the Gospel, as the name given to Jesus by the angel provided the opening bracket: 'They will call him "Emmanuel", a name which means "God is with us".' The divine presence of God in Jesus and in his community is the clue to the whole Gospel of Matthew. In the centre of the Gospel it is again stressed: 'Where two or three are gathered together in my name, there am I in the midst of them.'

Question: Why does Matthew present Jesus as the Second Moses? Does it mean anything to me?

In the evening of the first day of the week, the doors were closed in the room where the disciples were, for fear of the Jews. Jesus came and stood among them. He said to them, 'Peace be with you,' and showed them his hands and his side. The disciples were filled with joy when they saw the Lord, and he said to them again, 'Peace be with you.

'As the Father sent me,
so am I sending you.'
After saying this he breathed on them and said:
'Receive the Holy Spirit.
For those whose sins you forgive,
they are forgiven;
for those whose sins you retain,
they are retained.'

PENTECOST

The Gift of Peace

At first sight this is a surprising Gospel reading for Pentecost, but of course the event of Pentecost came too late to be a subject for the Gospels, and we read the account of another incident where the Risen Christ gave the Spirit to his disciples. There are two emphases in the account. The first is peace. Christ brings peace to his disciples with the double greeting of peace, and peace is a Christian watchword. Peace was the song of the angels at Jesus's birth. Each of Paul's letters opens with a greeting of peace. The letter to the Ephesians proclaims that Christ is our peace, the reversal of all worry, strife, envy, jealousy, self-seeking ambition. 'Go in peace' is Jesus's dismissal of those he cures, and also the dismissal at the end of Mass. Peace was Jesus's bequest to his disciples after the Last Supper. The second watchword is forgiveness, for God was always known as a God of mercy and forgiveness, as Jesus came to show by his constant approach to sinners. But the Lord's Prayer shows that if we do not ourselves forgive, we block God's forgiveness of ourselves too.

Question: 'Forgiveness is the only sure path to peace.' Does this cause any difficulties?

Jesus said to Nicodemus:

'God loved the world so much
that he gave his only Son,
so that everyone who believes in him may
    not be lost
but may have eternal life.
For God sent his Son into the world
not to condemn the world,
but so that through him the world might
    be saved.
No one who believes in him will be condemned;
but whoever refuses to believe is condemned
    already,
because he has refused to believe
in the name of God's only Son.

God so Loved the World

At first sight this part of the dialogue with Nicodemus seems to mention only the Father and the Son. A chief concern of the Gospel of John is to show the relationship of loving obedience between Father and Son. The love and equality in a perfect relationship between a human father and a son is the nearest reflection of such love which we can envisage. In complete trust and confidence father gives to son everything that is his. His only interest is the advancement of the son. The son's only care is to please his father and to be as close to his father as he can be, in word, action and relationships. Each has a vibrant and continuous bond of love for the other. Such a relationship may be rare in human family life, but it can model for us a pale reflection of the loving relationship between the Father and the Son. And the Spirit is in fact mentioned because the love itself is the living bond which unites the two. We must, however, appreciate that any such language belittles the divine relationship, which is of a different order of perfection and intensity. Human language can never begin to render the divine reality, which is utterly beyond our comprehension.

Question: What is the best human image for the Trinity?

Jesus said to the Jews:

> 'I am the living bread which has come down
>   from heaven.
> Anyone who eats this bread will live for ever;
> and the bread that I shall give
> is my flesh, for the life of the world.'

Then the Jews started arguing with one another: 'How can this man give us his flesh to eat?' they said. Jesus replied:

> 'I tell you most solemnly,
> if you do not eat the flesh of the Son of Man
> and drink his blood,
> you will not have life in you.
> Anyone who does eat my flesh and drink my blood
> has eternal life,
> and I shall raise him up on the last day.
> For my flesh is real food
> and my blood is real drink.
> He who eats my flesh and drinks my blood
> lives in me
> and I live in him.
> As I, who am sent by the living Father,
> myself draw life from the Father,
> so whoever eats me will draw life from me.
> This is the bread come down from heaven,
> not like the bread our ancestors ate:
> they are dead,
> but anyone who eats this bread will live for ever.'

The True Bread of Life

This is the final section of Jesus's great discourse in the Gospel of John on the Eucharist, delivered in the synagogue at Capernaum. It is in the form of a synagogue sermon, commenting in turn on the phrases of Psalm 78: 'He gave them bread - from heaven - to eat'. Jesus explains that these words are truly fulfilled not by Moses's historic gift of manna in the desert, but by the Father's continuous and repeated gift of Eucharistic bread. The discourse has the same pattern as the Mass: instruction followed by eating. The first two sections of the discourse were about God's gift of revelation in Christ, which is accepted and assimilated by belief in the teaching of Jesus. Now we come to the final section on God's gift of Christ as food. Particularly striking are two points. First, the stress on eating: the word used for '*eat* my flesh' is full of the reality of eating; it really means to 'chew', and designates the sacramental eating as a real assimilation of the nourishing food. The second point is that 'my flesh for the life of the world' links firmly to the Last Supper: the Christ that we receive is the Christ at the very moment of his redemptive act of self offering.

Question: How does Christ nourish us in the Eucharist?

Jesus instructed the Twelve as follows: 'Do not be afraid. For everything that is now covered will be uncovered, and everything now hidden will be made clear. What I say to you in the dark, tell in the daylight; what you hear in whispers, proclaim from the house-tops.

'Do not be afraid of those who kill the body but cannot kill the soul; fear him rather who can destroy both body and soul in hell. Can you not buy two sparrows for a penny? And yet not one falls to the ground without your Father knowing. Why, every hair on your head has been counted. So there is no need to be afraid; you are worth more than hundreds of sparrows.

'So if anyone declares himself for me in the presence of men, I will declare myself for him in the presence of my Father in heaven. But the one who disowns me in the presence of men, I will disown in the presence of my Father in heaven.'

Open and Fearless Speech

This whole chapter of Matthew brings together and sums up what Jesus has to say to his apostles about declaring his teaching in the face of hostility and persecution. Jesus himself was fearless in proclaiming his message. He 'taught with authority', as the Gospel constantly tells us. His disciples are sent out to do the same. We do not often meet with real persecution, though it may yet happen. The martyrs of communist Russia or Vietnam lived many years of peaceful Christianity before unexpectedly facing martyrdom. The monk martyrs of Algeria did not reckon on martyrdom when they went to Algeria. The only preparation for martyrdom can be fidelity and prayer. More often we face mockery for holding to Christian principles, and that too can be difficult to bear. We can be accused of narrow-mindedness, lack of appreciation of human values, blind obedience, sentimentality, naivety and a host of other hurtful slurs. Jesus did not promise that the Father would prevent the sparrows falling to the ground! Nor is it always easy to respond to such slurs with the patience and generosity as well as the truthfulness which Jesus would have shown. 'A spoonful of honey attracts more flies than a barrelful of vinegar,' said St Francis de Sales.

Question: Should I prepare for martyrdom? How?

Jesus instructed the Twelve as follows: 'Anyone who prefers father or mother to me is not worthy of me. Anyone who prefers son or daughter to me is not worthy of me. Anyone who does not take his cross and follow in my footsteps is not worthy of me. Anyone who finds his life will lose it; anyone who loses his life for my sake will find it.

'Anyone who welcomes you welcomes me; and those who welcome me welcome the one who sent me.

'Anyone who welcomes a prophet because he is a prophet will have a prophet's reward; and anyone who welcomes a holy man because he is a holy man will have a holy man's reward.

'If anyone gives so much as a cup of cold water to one of these little ones because he is a disciple, then I tell you solemnly, he will most certainly not lose his reward.'

Hardships of the Apostolate

At the end of this collection of sayings of Jesus about the mission of the Christian apostolate Matthew puts a whole series of daunting challenges. Luke gives almost all the same sayings, but scattered in different contexts. The last saying is only in Mark as well. Believing as we do that the composition of the Gospel is inspired, even to the selection and ordering of the sayings of Jesus, we can see this group of sayings as a series of challenges not to take up Christianity without serious forethought. There is no such thing as non-apostolic Christianity, but by becoming Christians we take on a share in Christ's own task of spreading the Good News. The challenge is great, but the reward is certain.

First comes a trio of sayings to show the absolute priority of Christ's claims, over the closest family ties, over life and finally over possession of one's own self. Then comes a quartet of promises of rewards to those who welcome Christ's messengers. The envoy is placed equal with the principal: Christ's messenger is as Christ, Christ as his Father. Then in detail the reward for welcome of a prophet, of any upright person, and finally of the Christian in need.

Question: What is the closest tie you have on earth? Can Jesus be more important than that?

Jesus exclaimed, 'I bless you, Father, Lord of heaven and of earth, for hiding these things from the learned and the clever and revealing them to mere children. Yes, Father, for that is what it pleased you to do. Everything has been entrusted to me by my Father; and no one knows the Son except the Father, just as no one knows the Father except the Son and those to whom the Son chooses to reveal him.

'Come to me, all you who labour and are overburdened, and I will give you rest. Shoulder my yoke and learn from me, for I am gentle and humble in heart, and you will find rest for your souls. Yes, my yoke is easy and my burden light.'

Father and Son

This much-loved and encouraging passage tells of the intimacy of the relationship between Father and Son in a way that no other passage of the synoptic Gospels does. It is reminiscent of those passages in John 5 which unfold the equality of Father and Son: the Son does nothing but what he sees the Father doing; the Father loves the Son so that he entrusts all things to the Son, and the Son gives life just as the Father gives life. Then comes the gentle invitation of the Son to all who are overburdened. The 'yoke' is often a symbol of the Law of Moses, which could seem burdensome with its many commands, though it was also valued as God's revelation of himself to his own people in love. Christ is not a tyrannical master, but is a sympathetic, gentle and humble leader who shares his life with his followers. The 'yoke' or Law of Christ, as we saw with regard to the second reading, is the interior impulse of the Spirit. It cannot be burdensome, since it is a joy to carry, a way of living with Christ and by his Spirit. Even the joy of martyrs, subjected as they are to physical pains, is a constant feature of accounts of martyrdom.

Question: What does Jesus mean by his 'yoke'? Do you find it comfortable?

Jesus left the house and sat by the lakeside, but such crowds gathered round him that he got into a boat and sat there. The people all stood on the beach, and he told them many things in parables.

He said, 'Imagine a sower going out to sow. As he sowed, some seeds fell on the edge of the path, and the birds came and ate them up. Others fell on patches of rock where they found little soil and sprang up straight away, because there was no depth of earth; but as soon as the sun came up they were scorched and, not having any roots, they withered away. Others fell among thorns, and the thorns grew up and choked them. Others fell on rich soil and produced their crop, some a hundredfold, some sixty, some thirty. Listen, anyone who has ears!'

The Parable of the Sower

Like any good teacher, Jesus uses pictures - or parables. Ever heard the one about the elephant and the wasp? Or electricity like a toy train going round a room? Anyway, for the next three weeks we have some of these pictures, to show us what Jesus is trying to do. This first one is rather sad. Whatever he does seems to fail: seed pecked up by birds, scorched by the sun, choked by thistles. What are my pecking birds, my scorching sun, my choking thistles which annihilate the seed Jesus sows in me? It is different for every one of us. But some, just a little, of the seed bears a fantastic harvest. There must be something I can show to the Lord with pride and gratitude: 'Look, this is the seed you gave me; it has grown, developed and here is your harvest.' Jesus, too, reflected on his mission to establish his Father's sovereignty on earth. Jesus, too, got depressed and wondered if he was getting anywhere. It was only when he had failed utterly, alone, deserted and tortured, that his perseverance won the crown. Jesus doesn't want the successful. He wants the failures as his followers - and that is where the harvest lies.

Question: Does this parable show Jesus as optimistic or disappointed?

(Longer form Matthew 13:1-23)

Jesus put another parable before the crowds: 'The kingdom of heaven may be compared to a man who sowed good seed in his field. While everybody was asleep his enemy came, sowed darnel all among the wheat, and made off. When the new wheat sprouted and ripened, the darnel appeared as well. The owner's servants went to him and said, "Sir, was it not good seed that you sowed in your field? If so, where does the darnel come from?" "Some enemy has done this" he answered. And the servants said, "Do you want us to go and weed it out?" But he said, "No, because when you weed out the darnel you might pull up the wheat with it. Let them both grow till the harvest; and at harvest time I shall say to the reapers: First collect the darnel and tie it in bundles to be burnt, then gather the wheat into my barn."'

The Kingdom of Heaven

The Gospel of Matthew gathers together a whole set of pictures which Jesus used to describe the society of God's servants which he was intent on setting up. Matthew calls it 'the Kingdom of Heaven'. Jews avoided bandying around the name of 'God', so Matthew calls it by the place where God is enthroned: heaven.

The first picture, the wheat and the darnel, shows that in some of those called the good seed has been overlaid by weed. In its early growth this weed, the inedible darnel, is incredibly difficult for a non farmer to distinguish from good barley. No more can we presume to sort out who is seeking God and who is not; it is dangerous to despise or to dismiss anyone at all. The explanation given by Matthew constitutes a warning that the harvest, the judgement, will come in the end.

The other two pictures form a pair. A mustard seed is a tiny grain, but shoots up in a few months to form a big bush. So a pinch of yeast makes a whole loaf of bread rise. Jesus could have told these to his disciples when they were depressed: 'Cheer up! Even a spark of goodwill can set a whole forest ablaze!'

Question: What do you learn from these parables about the Kingdom of God?

(Longer form Matthew 13:24-43)

Jesus said to the crowds: 'The kingdom of heaven is like treasure hidden in a field which someone has found; he hides it again, goes off happy, sells everything he owns and buys the field.

'Again, the kingdom of heaven is like a merchant looking for fine pearls; when he finds one of great value he goes and sells everything he owns and buys it.

'Again, the kingdom of heaven is like a dragnet cast into the sea that brings in a haul of all kinds. When it is full, the fishermen haul it ashore; then, sitting down, they collect the good ones in a basket and throw away those that are no use. This is how it will be at the end of time: the angels will appear and separate the wicked from the just to throw them into the blazing furnace where there will be weeping and grinding of teeth.

'Have you understood all this?' They said, 'Yes.' And he said to them, 'Well then, every scribe who becomes a disciple of the kingdom of heaven is like a householder who brings out from his storeroom things both new and old.'

Treasures New and Old

Three final pictures this week from Matthew's collection of Jesus's images of the Christian community. Matthew likes pairs of parables: the dragnet pairs with last week's darnel parable, the treasure pairs with the pearl. The Kingdom is an exciting and unexpected treasure which can change our whole life, like winning the pools or the lottery - except that God's gifts change us only for the good, and fill our lives with meaning and joy. Of course we know that God's call is demanding: you've got to pay a price for the field in which the treasure lies, or the genuine pearl found in a junkshop.

The very last picture - the householder bringing down different food packets, pots and jars off the shelf - is encouraging too: some are old favourites (perhaps the Christian values and prayers which we inherited from our families), but some add new flavours too, which we have discovered or been taught ourselves. If we listen, the Spirit is always there to show us new ways of living out our Christian calling, an opportunity for prayer or help or service. This 'householder' is often thought to be Matthew's own secret signature: he brings out old and new in the Christian message.

Question: Which is your favourite among all these images?

Jesus took with him Peter and James and his brother John and led them up a high mountain where they could be alone. There in their presence he was transfigured: his face shone like the sun and his clothes became as white as the light. Suddenly Moses and Elijah appeared to them; they were talking with him. Then Peter spoke to Jesus. 'Lord,' he said 'it is wonderful for us to be here; if you wish, I will make three tents here, one for you, one for Moses and one for Elijah.' He was still speaking when suddenly a bright cloud covered them with shadow, and from the cloud there came a voice which said, 'This is my Son, the Beloved; he enjoys my favour. Listen to him.' When they heard this, the disciples fell on their faces, overcome with fear. But Jesus came up and touched them. 'Stand up,' he said 'do not be afraid.' And when they raised their eyes they saw no one but only Jesus.

As they came down from the mountain Jesus gave them this order, 'Tell no one about the vision until the Son of Man has risen from the dead.'

The Transfiguration

Matthew's account is almost the same as Mark's. He adds the detail of Jesus's face shining like the sun. This was the case with Moses when he encountered God on the holy mountain, and Matthew, writing for Jewish Christians, is always keen to stress that Jesus was a Second Moses. He also changes the reaction of the disciples: in Mark they are so scared that they do not know what to say, but in Matthew they fall to the ground and do reverence, and Jesus gently raises them up.

Luke stresses that Jesus went up the mountain to pray. He frequently stresses Jesus's constant need for prayer, and many of Luke's parables are about prayer (the Importunate Widow and the Unjust Judge, the Pharisee and the Tax Collector). Luke also details that Jesus, Moses and Elijah were conversing about his journey up to Jerusalem, a journey which is the theme of the latter half of Luke's Gospel.

Jesus made the disciples get into the boat and go on ahead to the other side while he would send the crowds away. After sending the crowds away he went up into the hills by himself to pray. When evening came, he was there alone, while the boat, by now far out on the lake, was battling with a heavy sea, for there was a headwind. In the fourth watch of the night he went towards them, walking on the lake, and when the disciples saw him walking on the lake they were terrified. 'It is a ghost' they said, and cried out in fear. But at once Jesus called out to them, saying, 'Courage! It is I! Do not be afraid.' It was Peter who answered. 'Lord,' he said 'if it is you, tell me to come to you across the water.' 'Come' said Jesus. Then Peter got out of the boat and started walking towards Jesus across the water, but as soon as he felt the force of the wind, he took fright and began to sink. 'Lord! Save me!' he cried. Jesus put out his hand at once and held him. 'Man of little faith,' he said 'why did you doubt?' And as they got into the boat the wind dropped. The men in the boat bowed down before him and said, 'Truly, you are the Son of God.'

NINETEENTH SUNDAY IN ORDINARY TIME

Jesus and Peter on the Water

The Christian people are often depicted as a boat, with Peter at the helm. As in a boat, everyone has their part to play: kids to bring the excitement and the challenges, parents to take the responsibility, grandparents just to be there to comfort and reassure. Without Jesus they were getting exhausted, frustrated and probably bad tempered and quarrelling. When Jesus appears everything changes: first, terror and awed amazement, then Peter rushes to meet him - and loses confidence, only to be swiftly rescued. How does Jesus come to me? In the joys of family? In the unwelcome criticism of an angry neighbour who tells me the truth about myself? In the worries of a job or the agonies of a failed relationship? In the staggering beauty of creation? In physical pain? All these can bring God's presence, and without that presence we cannot expect to cope. Jesus does not force himself upon us. He just nudges us, and says: 'Here I am if you want me.' He may disappear into the sea mist again for a time, and we may sink into the water like mistrustful Peter. But it all ends with a welcome and a recognition that Jesus can cope even with a life-threatening situation.

Question: Why is Peter such a good role model for us?

Jesus left Gennesaret and withdrew to the region of Tyre and Sidon. Then out came a Canaanite woman from that district and started shouting, 'Sir, Son of David, take pity on me. My daughter is tormented by a devil.' But he answered her not a word. And his disciples went and pleaded with him. 'Give her what she wants,' they said 'because she is shouting after us.' He said in reply, 'I was sent only to the lost sheep of the House of Israel.' But the woman had come up and was kneeling at his feet. 'Lord,' she said 'help me.' He replied, 'It is not fair to take the children's food and throw it to the house-dogs.' She retorted, 'Ah yes, sir; but even house-dogs can eat the scraps that fall from their master's table.' Then Jesus answered her, 'Woman, you have great faith. Let your wish be granted.' And from that moment her daughter was well again.

Jesus and the Canaanite Woman

This is an especially significant scene in two ways. Mark's Gospel was the first to be written, and Matthew edits and expands it, using other sources as well. In Mark this scene is the only explicit encounter between Jesus and a gentile - and a woman at that! At first Jesus is reluctant to do anything for her, for his mission was primarily to Israel. He puts her off, and is really quite brusque with her. However, she wins through by her persistence and her determined confidence in his powers: the disciples get fed up with her shrieking after them, and ask Jesus to cure her daughter, which he does. We need to be persistent in our prayers and in our efforts. God does not grant a casual request. Secondly, it shows a lot about Jesus's relationship to women and about his sense of humour: they seem to tease each other with their repartee. There is the same repartee in the account of Jesus's meeting with the Samaritan woman in the Gospel of John: she stands up to him with her cheeky repartee. They are both obviously enjoying this playful scene. It suggests that not everything is solemn and serious in heaven, and there is room for a sense of humour!

Question: Is Jesus rude to the Canaanite woman, or is he merely challenging her?

When Jesus came to the region of Caesarea Philippi he put this question to his disciples, 'Who do people say the Son of Man is?' And they said, 'Some say he is John the Baptist, some Elijah, and others Jeremiah or one of the prophets.' 'But you,' he said, 'who do you say I am?' Then Simon Peter spoke up, 'You are the Christ,' he said 'the Son of the living God.' Jesus replied, 'Simon son of Jonah, you are a happy man! Because it was not flesh and blood that revealed this to you but my Father in heaven. So I now say to you: You are Peter and on this rock I will build my Church. And the gates of the underworld can never hold out against it. I will give you the keys of the kingdom of heaven: whatever you bind on earth shall be considered bound in heaven; whatever you loose on earth shall be considered loosed in heaven.' Then he gave the disciples strict orders not to tell anyone that he was the Christ.

Jesus Claims Peter as Rock

At last Peter recognises that Jesus is the Messiah, the Christ. At last he realises that in Jesus they can see the action of God. The disciples followed Jesus as soon as he called, but for a long time they were puzzled what to make of him, of his wonderful teaching and his godlike personality. Now comes a shaft of light and understanding. We too often take some time to appreciate the true worth of someone we know well: a little gesture can sometimes reveal just how generous and thoughtful they are. Peter suddenly grasps that there is God, acting among them, a daunting or even terrifying thought. Jesus replies to Peter's recognition with his own generosity, giving him a new name: 'Rock', for this is what 'Peter' means. If you name something, you make it your own, take it to yourself. This is just what Jesus does with Simon who becomes his own Peter. That is the importance of the naming of a child at Baptism: Jesus takes us to himself and we become his. The early Christians called themselves 'Those over whom the name of Jesus has been called.' We may have been named Mary or John, but the name of Jesus has been called over us and we have become his.

Question: What are the implications for us of Jesus's promise to Peter?

Jesus began to make it clear to his disciples that he was destined to go to Jerusalem and suffer grievously at the hands of the elders and chief priests and scribes, to be put to death and to be raised up on the third day. Then, taking him aside, Peter started to remonstrate with him. 'Heaven preserve you, Lord,' he said. 'This must not happen to you.' But he turned and said to Peter, 'Get behind me, Satan! You are an obstacle in my path, because the way you think is not God's way but man's.'

Then Jesus said to his disciples, 'If anyone wants to be a follower of mine, let him renounce himself and take up his cross and follow me. For anyone who wants to save his life will lose it; but anyone who loses his life for my sake will find it. What, then, will a man gain if he wins the whole world and ruins his life? Or what has a man to offer in exchange for his life?

'For the Son of Man is going to come in the glory of his Father with his angels, and, when he does, he will reward each one according to his behaviour.'

The Cross of Jesus

What a turn around! Last Sunday Peter was being congratulated on at last realising that Jesus was the Christ. He was promised the keys and authority to make decisions valid in heaven. Now Jesus shoos him away and tells him that he is Satan, the Tempter. Why the change? Jesus had told Peter that his role as Christ Messiah was to suffer and die in order to achieve his purpose, and Peter shied away from it. What is your particular soft option? What is the difficult task Christ is asking of you, and you avoiding? We are no better than his first disciples! In the Gospel this will happen twice more: three times Jesus foretells his passion and each time the disciples simply fail to understand. Each time Jesus again puts it bluntly that you cannot be a Christian without following Jesus in carrying a cross. We see people suffering the whole time, physical disabilities, breakdown of relationships, heartless treatment from others, financial worries - and then we grouse at a twinge of pain or a hurtful word. Carry the cross behind Jesus? Yes, of course I will, but if you don't mind, I'll just take that section which is well padded and fits my shoulder nicely. No point in unnecessary splinters in my neck.

Question: How does taking up our cross tally with 'My yoke is easy and my burden light'?

Jesus said to his disciples: 'If your brother does something wrong, go and have it out with him alone, between your two selves. If he listens to you, you have won back your brother. If he does not listen, take one or two others along with you: the evidence of two or three witnesses is required to sustain any charge. But if he refuses to listen to these, report it to the community; and if he refuses to listen to the community, treat him like a pagan or a tax collector.

'I tell you solemnly, whatever you bind on earth shall be considered bound in heaven; whatever you loose on earth shall be considered loosed in heaven.

'I tell you solemnly once again, if two of you on earth agree to ask anything at all, it will be granted to you by my Father in heaven. For where two or three meet in my name, I shall be there with them.'

Reconciliation

In working through the Gospel of Matthew for this year's readings the Church has had to be selective. In this eighteenth chapter of Matthew on relationships within the community it is striking that the Church has chosen this passage to put before us. The first part is all about sorting out disagreements and about forgiveness. Despite the presence of Christ in the Christian community there are going to be disagreements and misunderstandings in every community and every family. The vital thing is to sort them out and not to let them fester. So here we are given a safe process. Just afterwards, this is supplemented by Jesus's teaching that we have to forgive not just seven times (the perfect number) but seventy seven times. That means again and again and again, without limit.

We also get the reminder that Christ is present always in his community. The same promise is given at the beginning (the name *Emmanuel* means 'God with us') and the end of the Gospel ('I am with you to the end of time'). Therefore the decisions of the community will be considered binding in the sight of God. It is especially striking that the same promise is here given to the Church as had earlier been given to Peter himself. Peter on his own wields the authority of the Church.

Question: Would you add anything to this process of reconciliation?

Peter went up to Jesus and said, 'Lord, how often must I forgive my brother if he wrongs me? As often as seven times?' Jesus answered, 'Not seven, I tell you, but seventy-seven times.

'And so the kingdom of heaven may be compared to a king who decided to settle his accounts with his servants. When the reckoning began, they brought him a man who owed ten thousand talents; but he had no means of paying, so his master gave orders that he should be sold, together with his wife and children and all his possessions, to meet the debt. At this, the servant threw himself down at his master's feet. "Give me time," he said "and I will pay the whole sum." And the servant's master felt so sorry for him that he let him go and cancelled the debt. Now as this servant went out, he happened to meet a fellow servant who owed him one hundred denarii; and he seized him by the throat and began to throttle him. "Pay what you owe me," he said. His fellow servant fell at his feet and implored him, saying, "Give me time and I will pay you." But the other would not agree; on the contrary, he had him thrown into prison till he should pay the debt. His fellow servants were deeply distressed when they saw what had happened, and they went to their master and reported the whole affair to him. Then the master sent for him. "You wicked servant," he said "I cancelled all that debt of yours when you appealed to me. Were you not bound, then, to have pity on your fellow servant just as I had pity on you?" And in his anger the master handed him over to the torturers till he should pay all his debt. And that is how my heavenly Father will deal with you unless you each forgive your brother from your heart.'

The Unforgiving Debtor

This is a favourite parable of Matthew, continuing and concluding his theme that forgiveness is the life blood of any Christian community. We cannot live together without upsetting one another, unwittingly, or even deliberately. So forgiveness is the vital step. So important is it that two consecutive Sunday Gospels are devoted to it. It expands and stresses our petition in the Lord's Prayer: 'Forgive us our trespasses as we forgive others.' The importance of this petition was already underlined by Matthew; it is the only petition of the Lord's Prayer to which he adds at the end a confirmatory saying of Jesus. Like so many of Matthew's parables, this one revolves round contrasting characters, the 'goodie' and the 'baddie' (wedding guests and guest without a wedding garment; the two who use their talents and the one who hides it; the girls with and without oil for their lamps; the sheep and the goats). The contrast between the two sums of money is deliberately fantastic: the first slave owes millions of dollars, a sum no private person could ever repay, let alone a slave; it is more than a year's tax for a whole Roman province. The second owes a couple of months' wages of a casual labourer.

Question: Forgive and forget? Or can forgiveness become a bond of friendship?

Jesus told this parable to his disciples: 'The kingdom of heaven is like a landowner going out at daybreak to hire workers for his vineyard. He made an agreement with the workers for one denarius a day, and sent them to his vineyard. Going out at about the third hour he saw others standing idle in the market place and said to them, "You go to my vineyard too and I will give you a fair wage." So they went. At about the sixth hour and again at about the ninth hour, he went out and did the same. Then at about the eleventh hour he went out and found more men standing round, and he said to them, "Why have you been standing here idle all day?" "Because no one has hired us" they answered. He said to them, "You go into my vineyard too." In the evening, the owner of the vineyard said to his bailiff, "Call the workers and pay them their wages, starting with the last arrivals and ending with the first." So those who were hired at about the eleventh hour came forward and received one denarius each. When the first came, they expected to get more, but they too received one denarius each. They took it, but grumbled at the landowner. "The men who came last" they said "have done only one hour, and you have treated them the same as us, though we have done a heavy day's work in all the heat." He answered one of them and said, "My friend, I am not being unjust to you; did we not agree on one denarius? Take your earnings and go. I choose to pay the last-comer as much as I pay you. Have I no right to do what I like with my own? Why be envious because I am generous?" Thus the last will be first, and the first, last.'

The Payment of Wages

'It is not fair! They have hardly had time to roll up their sleeves, and the late comers get the same wage as I do, having sweated it out right through the heat of the day.'

OK, but God *is* unfair. What are you going to do about that?

'But they didn't deserve it, whereas I worked all day.'

OK, you worked. But how did you deserve even to exist?

'Well, God gave me existence, but he might at least be fair.'

OK, and where would that leave you, if God was fair and gave you what you deserve? Do you want a God in your own image, vengeful, scheming, lazy, punishing (other people), complacent, selfish?

'Hold on! Not completely like me, but at least I am *fair*.'

No. God isn't fair at all. That is why Jesus enjoyed having parties with sinners and people with whom you wouldn't be seen dead.

'Well, they will be different then, when they and I are dead - they'll be sort of cleaned up.'

Up to your standards, you mean? Are you sure God wants them 'cleaned up' like you? Perhaps God loves them just as much as you. Could Jesus ever have said: 'Blessed are the hungry and dirty and dishonest'?

Jesus said to the chief priests and the elders of the people, 'What is your opinion? A man had two sons. He went and said to the first, "My boy, you go and work in the vineyard today." He answered, "I will not go", but afterwards thought better of it and went. The man then went and said the same thing to the second who answered, "Certainly, sir", but did not go. Which of the two did the father's will?' 'The first' they said. Jesus said to them, 'I tell you solemnly, tax collectors and prostitutes are making their way into the kingdom of God before you. For John came to you, a pattern of true righteousness, but you did not believe him, and yet the tax collectors and prostitutes did. Even after seeing that, you refused to think better of it and believe in him.'

Parable of the Two Sons

Matthew loves giving parables of Jesus contrasting 'goodies' and 'baddies' like these two contrasting sons. Matthew's parables put everything in black and white terms with no shades of grey (wise and foolish wedding attendants, sheep and goats). Luke uses a different kind of parable, in which the characters - just like ourselves - often do the right thing for the wrong reason. The sayings of Jesus were handed down by word of mouth for some years before being written down. Did the straightforward contrast in Matthew (it is odd that both change their minds without a reason) develop into Luke's parable of the Prodigal Son? Both times the 'goodie' son ends up bad, and the 'baddie' son ends up good, but in Luke's version both changes of mind are motivated, and there is great emphasis on the son's repentance and the father's overwhelming joy at getting him back. The lesson in Matthew's story is given also by Jesus's word in the Sermon on the Mount: 'It is not anyone who says to me, "Lord, Lord" who will enter the Kingdom of Heaven, but the person who does the will of my Father in Heaven'. It is no use simply saying that Christ is our 'Lord', we have to express it in our behaviour.

Question: What does this say about hypocrisy in religion?

Jesus said to the chief priests and the elders of the people, 'Listen to another parable. There was a man, a landowner, who planted a vineyard; he fenced it round, dug a winepress in it and built a tower; then he leased it to tenants and went abroad. When vintage time drew near he sent his servants to the tenants to collect his produce. But the tenants seized his servants, thrashed one, killed another and stoned a third. Next he sent some more servants, this time a larger number, and they dealt with them in the same way. Finally he sent his son to them. "They will respect my son" he said. But when the tenants saw the son, they said to each other, "This is the heir. Come on, let us kill him and take over his inheritance." So they seized him and threw him out of the vineyard and killed him. Now when the owner of the vineyard comes, what will he do to those tenants?' They answered, 'He will bring those wretches to a wretched end and lease the vineyard to other tenants who will deliver the produce to him when the season arrives.' Jesus said to them, 'Have you never read in the scriptures:

> It was the stone rejected by the builders
> that became the keystone.
> This was the Lord's doing
> and it is wonderful to see?

'I tell you, then, that the kingdom of God will be taken from you and given to a people who will produce its fruit.'

Wicked Tenants of the Vineyard

Jesus's understanding of the sovereignty of God brought him the violent opposition of some of the Jewish leaders. Were they corrupt, or just closed to any new way of thinking, so closed that they could not see that Jesus was the promised Messiah? Anyway, Jesus used this story about the tenants of a vineyard to show that they were not leading the people as they should. Everyone would immediately understand the image of the vineyard. The prophet Isaiah - and many others after him - had used this image in a well-known poem eight centuries earlier to show that the vineyard of Israel refused to yield a good harvest to God, whatever care God lavished on it. God expected *fairness of judgement* and all he found was a *shriek of agony* (the same word in Hebrew apart from one letter). What does this mean for us? Not that we have to follow every new idea. But it does mean that we must be open to the idea that we may be wrong, that our service of the Lord may be faulty, that people we find tiresome or unacceptable may have more good in them than we credit them with. God's ways are not our ways, and we need to watch out for the bend in the road.

Question: Are the tenants of God's Christian vineyard any better than the previous tenants? Who are they, anyway?

Jesus said to the chief priests and elders of the people: 'The kingdom of heaven may be compared to a king who gave a feast for his son's wedding. He sent his servants to call those who had been invited, but they would not come. Next he sent some more servants. "Tell those who have been invited" he said "that I have my banquet all prepared, my oxen and fattened cattle have been slaughtered, everything is ready. Come to the wedding." But they were not interested: one went off to his farm, another to his business, and the rest seized his servants, maltreated them and killed them. The king was furious. He despatched his troops, destroyed those murderers and burnt their town. Then he said to his servants, "The wedding is ready; but as those who were invited proved to be unworthy, go to the crossroads in the town and invite everyone you can find to the wedding." So these servants went out on to the roads and collected together everyone they could find, bad and good alike; and the wedding hall was filled with guests. When the king came in to look at the guests he noticed one man who was not wearing a wedding garment, and said to him, "How did you get in here, my friend, without a wedding garment?" And the man was silent. Then the king said to the attendants, "Bind him hand and foot and throw him out into the dark, where there will be weeping and grinding of teeth." For many are called, but few are chosen.'

The Wedding Banquet

A wedding is a time of joy and completion after long preparation, a time of love and of complete satisfaction. In Judaism at the time of Jesus the coming of the Messiah is often compared to a wedding feast. The Marriage Feast at Cana must have been some party! At Mary's request Jesus produced nine hundred litres of wine. The Letter to the Ephesians teaches that the love in a human wedding is only a pale shadow of Christ's love for his bride, the Church. In this story of the royal wedding, however, two things go drastically wrong. First, the original wedding guests refuse to come. Not only do they refuse, but they brutally maltreat the innocent messengers, and the King (who must stand for God) relentlessly burns down their city. This must be an adjustment to Jesus's story, applying it to the Sack of Jerusalem, captured and burnt by the Romans in AD 70, a few years before Matthew was writing. Secondly, the man who has no wedding garment is slung out. A wedding garment is a standard Jewish image for works of generosity expected of every faithful Jew. For us Christians, too, the story constitutes a double warning.

Question: Are we alert and listening for God's call? Do we rest secure in being called Christians and leave the dirty jobs to others?

The Pharisees went away to work out between them how to trap Jesus in what he said. And they sent their disciples to him, together with the Herodians, to say, 'Master, we know that you are an honest man and teach the way of God in an honest way, and that you are not afraid of anyone, because a man's rank means nothing to you. Tell us your opinion, then. Is it permissible to pay taxes to Caesar or not?' But Jesus was aware of their malice and replied, 'You hypocrites! Why do you set this trap for me? Let me see the money you pay the tax with.' They handed him a denarius, and he said, 'Whose head is this? Whose name?' 'Caesar's' they replied. He then said to them, 'Very well, give back to Caesar what belongs to Caesar – and to God what belongs to God.'

The Question of Taxes

They must really have thought they had their victim sewn up! If Jesus said he paid the Roman taxes, he recognised the Emperor, not God, as his Lord. If he said he didn't pay, he was a traitor to Rome. Jesus turns the question back on them. First he makes them admit that they themselves recognise Rome as overlord by carrying a Roman coin, for the coin would carry the Emperor's head. Next he puts to them a question: what do *they* consider is due to Caesar? Finally he goes beyond their question, to interrogate their ultimate loyalty: in the last analysis, just what is due to God? At a superficial level this seems a little verbal tussle, in which Jesus outwits his opponents. But the story was remembered and passed on in the Christian community not because of Jesus's cleverness, but because at a deeper level it is a question which Jesus puts to each of us: just where do our loyalties and priorities lie? Money? Respect? Sex? Fame? A good holiday? Comfort? Power? Jesus is not a dictator who imposes his will. He just asks the question and leave us to give our own answer. To those who question him he gives no easy answer, but always replies with another question.

Question: Where do my priorities lie - money, sex, power, fame, leisure?

When the Pharisees heard that Jesus had silenced the Sadducees they got together and, to disconcert him, one of them put a question, 'Master, which is the greatest commandment of the Law?' Jesus said, 'You must love the Lord your God with all your heart, with all your soul, and with all your mind. This is the greatest and the first commandment. The second resembles it: you must love your neighbour as yourself. On these two commandments hang the whole Law, and the Prophets also.'

The Greatest Commandment

Familiarity with Jesus's answer to the question about the greatest commandment blunts our awareness of its startling directness. Answers could be given, singling out one of the ten commandments as the greatest, the most important basis of society. A frequent answer to the question was and is the Golden Rule, existing in many cultures: 'Do not do to another what you would not have done to you'. This is basically a selfish answer, protecting my own interests. By contrast, Jesus's answer slams home, turning away from self to God. 'Love', not 'obey' or 'adore' or 'fear' or 'reverence'. Love is not the warmth of companionship or of sex, but is the willing generosity of a mother to a helpless young child or a daughter to a helpless old parent, of a wife to an alcoholic husband or a husband to a paralysed wife, seeking no reward, but the happiness of the recipient. Paul gives a useful checklist in 1 Corinthians 13. The First Letter of John gives a shorter checklist: 'No one who fails to love the brother or sister whom he can see, can love God whom he has not seen'. The real interests of the recipient of love may not always be easy to find, but the spirit of giving is unmistakable.

Question: Whom do you know who really practises the commandment of love?

Addressing the people and his disciples Jesus said, 'The scribes and the Pharisees occupy the chair of Moses. You must therefore do what they tell you and listen to what they say; but do not be guided by what they do: since they do not practise what they preach. They tie up heavy burdens and lay them on men's shoulders, but will they lift a finger to move them? Not they! Everything they do is done to attract attention, like wearing broader phylacteries and longer tassels, like wanting to take the place of honour at banquets and the front seats in the synagogues, being greeted obsequiously in the market squares and having people call them Rabbi.

'You, however, must not allow yourselves to be called Rabbi, since you have only one Master, and you are all brothers. You must call no one on earth your father, since you have only one Father, and he is in heaven. Nor must you allow yourselves to be called teachers, for you have only one Teacher, the Christ. The greatest among you must be your servant. Anyone who exalts himself will be humbled, and anyone who humbles himself will be exalted.'

The Scribes and Pharisees Denounced

This is the fiercest of all the hard things which the Gospel of Matthew has to say about the scribes and Pharisees. It introduces a sevenfold curse upon them. The Pharisees were the party of the Jews most concerned for the exact observance of the prescriptions of the Law of Moses. The 'scribes' were lawyers to whom they would turn in the case of a clash between two laws. Their attention to detail and their fussiness often made them lose sight of the real purpose of the Law. However, Jesus was prepared to meet them on the Pharisees' own ground and debate with them in their own terms. In the Gospels, and especially in Matthew, written towards the end of the century, the hostility to this group has obviously become fiercer, no doubt because of their persecution of the followers of Jesus. As Matthew warns: 'they will flog you in their synagogues.' One of their concerns was obviously the status of the religious leaders. It looks as though they were turning into little gods on their own. So here the Gospel stresses by contrast that all the disciples of Jesus are equal: in Christianity there is only one Father, only one teacher for all.

Question: Should we use titles such as 'Father' within our Christian practice?

Jesus told this parable to his disciples: 'The kingdom of heaven will be like this: Ten bridesmaids took their lamps and went to meet the bridegroom. Five of them were foolish and five were sensible: the foolish ones did take their lamps, but they brought no oil, whereas the sensible ones took flasks of oil as well as their lamps. The bridegroom was late, and they all grew drowsy and fell asleep. But at midnight there was a cry, "The bridegroom is here! Go out and meet him." At this, all those bridesmaids woke up and trimmed their lamps, and the foolish ones said to the sensible ones, "Give us some of your oil: our lamps are going out." But they replied, "There may not be enough for us and for you; you had better go to those who sell it and buy some for yourselves." They had gone off to buy it when the bridegroom arrived. Those who were ready went in with him to the wedding hall and the door was closed. The other bridesmaids arrived later. "Lord, Lord," they said "open the door for us." But he replied, "I tell you solemnly, I do not know you." So stay awake, because you do not know either the day or the hour.'

The Ten Wedding Attendants

Of course they weren't *bride*smaids! According to the custom of the time the girls were attendant on the bride*groom*, to greet him with their lamps as he arrived at the wedding reception. Anyway, half of them weren't ready, let him down, and then found themselves shut out. There is a subtle difference between the parables given in Mark's and Matthew's Gospels. In Mark they are all about the sudden coming of God's Kingship in history, at the time of Jesus. Jesus proclaimed that the crisis was *now*. In him God's reign had arrived: it was time to take drastic action. Matthew's parables take a longer-term view: there will be a final judgement at the end of time, for which we, in the Church and in the course of history, must prepare. Some will, some won't. Some will be found to be wheat, others to be weeds. When the catch of fish comes in, some fish will be thrown away, some kept. Some will be sheep and others goats. Each year, as the liturgical year draws to a close, the Church reminds us of this. And it will be sudden and unpredictable, like a burglar on the one night I forgot to lock the door, or like a mousetrap snapping shut, or like the unpredictable moment of birthpangs.

Question: Can't I just forget about the whole thing? I am not going to die tomorrow.

Jesus spoke this parable to his disciples: 'The kingdom of heaven is like a man on his way abroad who summoned his servants and entrusted his property to them. To one he gave five talents, to another two, to a third one; each in proportion to his ability. Then he set out.

Now a long time after, the master of those servants came back and went through his accounts with them. The man who had received the five talents came forward bringing five more. "Sir," he said "you entrusted me with five talents; here are five more that I have made."

A Story about Talents

It is encouraging to think of all the talents which friends and neighbours have and which I don't have. It is all part of the gifts of the Spirit, which Paul sees as making up the whole Body of Christ. Everyone has a special contribution to make. As for me, it is extraordinary that God created me with all my twists, defects, fears and failures, and it is precisely because of those boils, sores, abscesses that God loves me, helps me and guides me to work out my salvation. And it is just possible that there may be friends who can think that God has given me talents which make a tiny contribution to the happiness and goodness of the world. What of the man who has only one 'talent', digs it into the earth, and is so severely treated? This is surely someone who resolutely turns his (or her) back on the goodness she (or he) has received and refuses to work with it for the Lord's purposes or anyone else's. Such a talent goes to waste and merely rusts and corrupts. If I know anyone like that it is just worth asking whether, with infinite and patient kindness, I can just help that person to release the talent and bring it to blossom.

Question: What are your chief talents and how do you use them?

(Longer form Matthew 25:14-30)

Jesus said to his disciples: 'When the Son of Man comes in his glory, escorted by all the angels, then he will take his seat on his throne of glory. All the nations will be assembled before him and he will separate men one from another as the shepherd separates sheep from goats. He will place the sheep on his right hand and the goats on his left. Then the King will say to those on his right hand, "Come, you whom my Father has blessed, take for your heritage the kingdom prepared for you since the foundation of the world. For I was hungry and you gave me food; I was thirsty and you gave me drink; I was a stranger and you made me welcome; naked and you clothed me, sick and you visited me, in prison and you came to see me." Then the virtuous will say to him in reply, "Lord, when did we see you hungry and feed you; or thirsty and give you drink? When did we see you a stranger and make you welcome; naked and clothe you; sick or in prison and go to see you?" And the King will answer, "I tell you solemnly, in so far as you did this to one of the least of these brothers of mine, you did it to me." Next he will say to those on his left hand, "Go away from me, with your curse upon you, to the eternal fire prepared for the devil and his angels. For I was hungry and you never gave me food; I was thirsty and you never gave me anything to drink; I was a stranger and you never made me welcome, naked and you never clothed me, sick and in prison and you never visited me." Then it will be their turn to ask, "Lord, when did we see you hungry or thirsty, a stranger or naked, sick or in prison, and did not come to your help?" Then he will answer, "I tell you solemnly, in so far as you neglected to do this to one of the least of these, you neglected to do it to me." And they will go away to eternal punishment, and the virtuous to eternal life.'

OUR LORD JESUS CHRIST, KING OF THE UNIVERSE

The Last Judgement

This is the last of Matthew's great parables. The world is finally divided into 'goodies' and 'baddies'. The great dramatic scene here depicted will not necessarily happen all at once, but we shall each of us at the moment of death face the judgement of our divine Lord in his glory. This confrontation will be an experience far more awesome and shattering than any description can express, and yet fulfilling and re-assuring. We will know at last in a naked way our own filth and also our own infinite value to this transcendent figure.

Two striking points are stressed in the parable. First, we will be judged uniquely on our treatment of those in any kind of need. Not on our prayer life. Not on our asceticism or penances undertaken. Only on our respect for others, how far we look to see what they need and what we can give. Each of the Ten Commandments in the Old Testament, each of the eight beatitudes in the New can be reduced to this: telling the truth, financial honesty, honouring father and mother (or children), hunger for justice, peace making. The second striking point is the reason for the first: that Christ is in each person. What we do to others, we do to Christ.

Question: What does it really mean that Christ is in myself and all other people?

The Jerusalem Bible translation

The Jerusalem Bible was first published in 1966. It was produced by a team of distinguished English scholars (including J.R.R. Tolkien), working under Alexander Jones. It made available for English readers the findings of the French Bible de Jérusalem published a decade earlier by the famous French biblical school in Jerusalem, the first Catholic Bible edition to incorporate all the advances of modern biblical study. The Jerusalem Bible was the first translation of the whole Bible into modern English, and as such has maintained its status as authorised for use in the liturgy.

Acknowledgements

CTS gratefully acknowledges Bloomsbury for their permission to reproduce some of Fr Wansbrough's material in this publication.

Images: Page 3: Icon of St Matthew on the presbytery door in St. Constantine and Helena church, Bruges, Belgium. © Renata Sedmakova / Shutterstock.com

Page 38: Miraculous conversion of the Samaritan woman © Zvonimir Atletic

Page 44: The Raising of Lazarus, Russian icon, Novgorod School, 15th century (tempera on panel) / Museum of Art, Novgorod, Russia / Bridgeman Images

Page 58: Image of Christ on the Great Meteoron Monastery stairs © Netfalls - Remy Musser